Palgrave Studies in Comedy

Series Editors
Roger Sabin
University of the Arts London
London, UK

Sharon Lockyer
Brunel University
London, UK

Comedy is part of the cultural landscape as never before, as older manifestations such as performance (stand-up, plays, etc.), film and TV have been joined by an online industry, pioneered by YouTube and social media. This innovative new book series will help define the emerging comedy studies field, offering fresh perspectives on the comedy studies phenomenon, and opening up new avenues for discussion. The focus is 'pop cultural', and will emphasize vaudeville, stand-up, variety, comedy film, TV sit-coms, and digital comedy. It will welcome studies of politics, history, aesthetics, production, distribution, and reception, as well as work that explores international perspectives and the digital realm. Above all it will be pioneering – there is no competition in the publishing world at this point in time.

More information about this series at
http://www.palgrave.com/gp/series/14644

Susanne Colleary

The Comic
Everywoman in Irish
Popular Theatre

Political Melodrama, 1890-1925

Susanne Colleary
Institute of Technology Sligo
Sligo, Ireland

Palgrave Studies in Comedy
ISBN 978-3-030-02007-1   ISBN 978-3-030-02008-8   (eBook)
https://doi.org/10.1007/978-3-030-02008-8

Library of Congress Control Number: 2018962556

This Palgrave Macmillan imprint is published by the registered company Springer Nature Switzerland AG
The registered company address is: Gewerbestrasse 11, 6330 Cham, Switzerland

For my father Eddie with the nut brown hair, we will meet you on the bridge

CONTENTS

LIST OF FIGURES

CHAPTER 1

Front Cloth

Abstract The Front Cloth sets out its stall for the work. It introduces the reader to the shape of the book, which begins by tracing the socio-historical and cultural contexts that informed the world of the popular plays in Ireland. It speaks briefly to melodramatic aesthetics, and it outlines the dual approaches of academic and practice-as-research strands of analysis that form the spine of the book. It sketches the performance possibilities of Irish comic women on popular stages. It outlines the nature and function of the comic everywoman as a means to recognise comic women and their audiences in popular theatre during some of the most turbulent years in Irish history.

Keywords Patriotic • Melodrama • Theatre • Comedy • Comic Everywoman

This book is born of a love of comedy and performance. It takes as its focus Irish political melodrama as mass entertainment through the late nineteenth and into the first decades of the twentieth century in Ireland. The timeframe encapsulates some of the most turbulent years in recent Irish history, incorporating as it does the growing struggle to gain independence from British rule. The study dates are an attempt to capture those years, offering a broad historical guideline, and in that respect, they create the shape for the work. Tackling comedy when nationalist

© The Author(s) 2018
S. Colleary, *The Comic Everywoman in Irish Popular Theatre*,
Palgrave Studies in Comedy,
https://Doi.org/10.1007/978-3-030-02008-8_1

politics are in the same sentence can be difficult. Those discourses kept pulling away from the comic elements for some time, because the nationalist emblem is writ so large through the plays and reflected in the breadth and depth of cultural work about this period in Irish history. Those debates and controversies are well rehearsed elsewhere, and it would do little good to repeat what others have done far better than I. Necessarily, the work begins by tracing the historical, cultural and theatrical contexts of the period, within which the patriotic plays lived; those contexts inform and scaffold the remainder of the book. However, this book represents an exploration into the world of the patriotic melodramas in a related but different way. Moving on from those contextualised brushstrokes, the book makes enquiry of melodramatic worlds, its aesthetics as performance on both sides of the Irish Sea, with some discussion of the cultural anxieties surrounding its popularity on Irish stages. It does so in order to direct the enquiry towards *alternative* comic possibilities for the playtexts as popular theatre, while building on the substantive work of those who have already established the native dramas as significant in Irish political and cultural history.

Approaching the work from a comedy studies perspective was rewarding and challenging in the same measure. Extracting the comic structures from the plays was invigorating and laborious; the plays are built in soap opera repetition and for me, for some time at least, impossible to fully catch hold of. This is in part due to the familiarity of plot and motive, which can meld, but also because, in my view, the texts serve as a key; in other words, the plays only really come to life as performance. I acknowledge the bias while also suggesting that the idea is helped by the ways in which the plays came into the world; they are not born of a literary or 'writerly' tradition. Reading them, however much you like them, can make you forget, *playing* them makes you remember. And written as they were by actor-managers for performance, and as popular entertainments they had a ready market in Dublin, along the theatrical axis, and in the 'smalls,' which toured the rural towns of Ireland. So this study became about the comedy in the works and the working of that comedy through the totality of the performance text. It also became about practice and performance, and both approaches are detailed in this book. The academic study concentrates on in-depth, comic analysis of four of the patriotic plays, by the playwrights J.W. Whitbread and P.J. Bourke, as exemplary of their type, while also signalling to the works of those who had gone before, including Dion Boucicault and Hubert O'Grady. The selected plays evolved with the new decades of the twentieth century and the rising political and cultural tensions in Ireland. The analysis draws out the comic women while the practice-as-research enquiry offers new insights into their performance, with emphasis on staged comic women. Having separated out the approaches, it is important to note that they fold back in on each other; they are interwoven, with the discussion building from both, either in parallel or simultaneously. At the nexus of both approaches is a loose association of ideas, which I have called the comic everywoman. What became the comic everywoman started out with an arc of research that worked from broad understanding of the nature and function of the patriotic plays to the comedy at work in the plays to the comic women at work in the plays. Focussing in on the comic women deepened the direction of the study towards female comic agency on the popular stage: its freedoms and its constraints. The enquiry became about that mediated space for comic women, and what it might allow. The practice-as-research approach both on its own terms and speaking dialectically to the academic work goes some way to sketching how comic women had access to power within that inverted space of play. Both approaches also examine those inversions as the means to capture ways of playing that went beyond the text. The comic everywoman then is built out of the familiarity of stock, performing twice nightly for thousands of men and women and staging comic identity that has the means to play out versions of the *performance text* in relationship with, and to, her audience. This is the centre of the book and represents its beginning only. The formulation is proposed as a way for the comic women of distant texts and on popular stages in Ireland to be, as Cathy Leeney would say, seen and heard; for me, that is what is most exciting about it.

CHAPTER 2

Popular Theatre in Ireland

Abstract This chapter sketches the broad historical and socio-political contexts that inform the world of popular theatre in the years surrounding the 1916 Rising in Dublin. The work considers the Queen's Theatre as the 'Home of Irish Drama' in relationship to its audiences and to the wider theatrical landscape in Dublin. The chapter then moves on to consider the melodramatic aesthetic and its uses in the Irish patriotic plays, in order to understand how the political plays worked as performance. It makes discussion of the cultural anxieties surrounding the plays then and now, and it signals out to the work of the remaining chapters, placing comic women in Irish popular performance as central to the study.

Keywords Queen's • Nationalism • Political • Theatre • Melodrama • Acting • Audience

2.1 BRUSHSTROKES

There was no shortage of entertainment for those out and about for the evening in late nineteenth-century Dublin, where the theatrical landscape was bountiful and eclectic. Dublin then housed three patented theatres, licensed to produce drama, the Queen's Royal Theatre, the Gaiety Theatre and the Theatre Royal. In 1871, brothers Michael and John Gunn opened

© The Author(s) 2018
S. Colleary, *The Comic Everywoman in Irish Popular Theatre*,
Palgrave Studies in Comedy,
https://doi.org/10.1007/978-3-030-02008-8_2

the Gaiety Theatre in Dublin, declaiming their intent to "give the public in Dublin the best in Variety and excellence the world can afford."[1] In 1874, the brothers took over the controlling interest at the Theatre Royal and ran it as a touring house in much the same vein as the Gaiety.[2] Typical entertainments at the Gaiety included offerings of Shakespeare, Goldsmith, Sheridan and Wilde, while the operas of Wagner, Verdi, Bizet and Gilbert and O'Sullivan were also popular. Farces and romantic and/or musical comedies were also well received.[3] Not far away the Queen's Royal Theatre, under the directorship of Arthur Lloyd, "increasingly presented Music-Hall fare—comic turns, songs and performing animals."[4] Christopher Morash notes that touring companies were also becoming more popular, "playing Belfast, Cork and sometimes Limerick or Waterford,' [constituting] the Irish theatrical axis."[5] The circuit was attractive to English companies at the time, following rail lines as well as older established theatrical routes, which for practical reasons, including poor transport links, tended to exclude the midlands and the west of the country. Morash notes that as the end of the century approached, the time lag between London openings and Irish touring dates narrowed, so that Irish audiences were appreciating Gilbert and Sullivan or Pinero not long after their English counterparts. He also makes the point that plays written about Ireland by Irish playwrights, including the works of Dion Boucicault and Hubert O'Grady, often opened in England or America, only coming to Ireland as part of the touring circuit.[6]

The road less travelled was accommodated by the 'fit ups' or 'smalls'—bands of travelling players who performed from town to town up and down the country.[7] While the performance histories of the fit ups are underwritten in Irish academia, what is known is that they existed at least from the early nineteenth century onwards. The oldest and most famous of the troupes arguably were the J.B. Carrickford Company and Tommy Conway (or Keegan), who formed the Bohemian Minstrels in the late 1800s.[8] Others included the Anew McMaster Company, which began before the 1920s. Typically the travelling companies:

> … carried all their props, scenery, costumes, curtains and light system … and if necessary the materials for a temporary improvised stage which they would fit-up in whatever sort of venue was available.[9]

According to Philip Ryan, the number of companies grew steadily from a scattering to a sizable number in the first decades of the twentieth century, with Morash also noting their prevalence, "roaming the countryside, playing everywhere from the Curragh Army Camp to church halls in Sligo."[10] Ryan estimates that by the 1930s, as many as 60 companies were touring the small towns and villages around Ireland, establishing a distinct entertainment style. The fit-up performance tradition could typically include variety acts, and melodrama (either a stock favourite or a 'potted' version of a contemporaneous film or book), often ending with a 'laughable' or 'screaming' farce.[11] The coming of the First World War, while a difficult period for all of Dublin's theatres, was to prove in certain respects advantageous to those who primarily worked the fit ups. Conscription and travelling restrictions made it almost impossible for overseas performers to honour commitments, and increasingly from 1916 onwards, Irish performers attempted to bridge the gap. The booking agent Charlie Jones tried to facilitate all:

> I kept a 'nest' of artists together in Dublin and would assemble them every Monday morning while awaiting the usual urgent messages from theatres in Dublin Cork, Belfast, Limerick and other places that so-and-so had failed to turn up ... and always managed to complete the dates this way.[12]

While the theatres struggled to keep their doors open, events brought with it an upsurge of Irish drama aided by the many amateur theatre companies formed during the period, the best of which appeared at the Queen's and at the Theatre Royal.[13] Hogan and Burnham note, somewhat superficially, that before the war the Queen's had imported English touring company staples to provide "stirring or sentimental melodramas about American cowboys and Lancashire mill girls."[14] Irish companies stepped into the breach, more attuned though they were to playing the 'smalls,' and only occasionally performing in Dublin.[15] Cheryl Herr makes the interesting point that the war put some of those companies to the pin of their stock performance collar. What went down well in rural Ireland was now to some extent having to play out successfully in Dublin, creating a timely performance synergy for ideas of Irish identity and representation on both urban and rural stages.[16]

2.2   PLAYING POLITICS AT THE QUEEN'S— BOUCICAULT'S ECHO

In 1884 the Queen's came under new management when the British playwright and entrepreneur J.W. Whitbread took over, beginning what Séamus de Búrca describes as its golden age, and ending in 1907 with his retirement.[17] From that beginning, the theatre began to clearly identify itself with 'native drama' and broad nationalist sentiment, then popular with Dublin working and middle-class audiences. Whitbread also began making changes to the Queen's stylistics. He staged his own play productions as well as touring them as far as Australia and the United States and his cycle of plays commemorating Irish heroes of the failed 1798 rebellion against the Crown played well to Irish and British audiences.[18] As a receiving house he also emphasised hosting Irish plays from overseas including the work of Limerick-born Irish playwright Hubert O'Grady as well as reviving the mid to late nineteenth-century popular Irish melodramas, with the master Dion Boucicault as stalwart. For Stephen Watt, by the turn of the century, the theatre had achieved a fairly consistent fare of melodrama, whether from touring companies or in-house revivals and openings so that:

> ... some fifteen to seventeen weeks ... in a production calendar abbreviated only by Holy Week or more typically by longer four to six week Lenten closings, was filled by Irish dramas by Boucicault, Buckstone, Cooke O'Grady or Whitbread.[19]

According to Ben Levitas, O'Grady's early career (both he and his wife were actors in Boucicault's troop) as a playwright was borrowed clothes from Boucicault's melodramatic style including generating "a romantic whiff for Fenian charm while securing a comedic restoration of social strata."[20] However he adds that O'Grady engineered melodramatic convention towards more overt political commentary in his trilogy: *The Eviction* (1879–80), *Emigration* (1883) and *The Famine* (1886), which were perennial favourites at the theatre until the late 1920s.[21] As with O'Grady, Boucicault also ghosts Whitbread's work and both Mary Trotter and Herr place his play structures within a Boucicaultian style of writing. Watt and Herr suggest that Boucicault's last play, the more politicised *Robert Emmet*, transitioned the form towards a Whitbreadian style with a more radicalised representation of character and plot.[22] In particular, Christopher Fitz-Simon also maps *Robert Emmet* onto Whitbread's history plays as "tales, which had an acknowledged national hero as the eponymous leading figure—a Hibernian biopic before the invention of the commercial cinema."[23] Current scholarship, however, has questioned Boucicault's authorship of the piece, and Deirdre McFeely makes strong argument for Frank Marshall as the principal writer of the play.[24] That said, Whitbread's Hibernian biopics also include *Lord Edward Fitzgerald* (1894), *Theobald Wolfe Tone*

(1898), *Rory O'More* (an adaptation of an earlier Samuel Lover play) (1900), *The Insurgent Chief* (1902), *The Ulster Hero* (1903) and *Sarsfield* (1904).[25]
The Queen's theatre closed for renovations in March 1907, not reopening its doors until September 1909. With Whitbread gone, Herr notes that the new management were exponents of British sensationalist melodrama, pantomime and variety acts, but did on occasion run the Irish plays.[26] Not until the arrival of actor-manager and playwright P.J. Bourke in and around 1910 did the Queen's clearly reorient itself again towards the political melodramas. Bourke and others along with him, perhaps most significantly another actor-manager and playwright Ira Allen, strengthened the tradition for the patriotic plays at the Queen's.[27] Morash makes the point well:

> ... just as the plays of Whitbread (and to an even greater extent, Hubert O'Grady) moved away from the conciliatory endings of Boucicault, and his predecessors, Bourke's plays take a further step toward unappeasable militancy.[28]

Herr describes Bourke as the poster boy for the times, "politically passionate, thoroughly theatrical, socially aware," his time at the theatre "brought patriotic Irish melodrama to its most pertinent form."[29] His No. 1 Company had played outside the Queen's before 1910, with Bourke's first professional production of his '98 drama *When Wexford Rose* appearing there in 1912. Ira Allen's most popular play remained *Father Murphy* (1919) with the theatre staging revivals of Boucicault, O'Grady and Whitbread. Bourke's melodramas include *Kathleen Mavourneen* (as adaptation) (1907), *The Northern Insurgents* (1912), *In Dark and Evil Days* (1914) and *For Ireland's Liberty* (1914). In 1915 Bourke staged his play *For The Land She Loved* at W.B. Yeats' and Lady Gregory's influential Abbey Theatre. The play was billed as a benefit for the Defence of Ireland Fund in James Connolly's newspaper, *The Workers' Republic*. At the time, the British Government was coming down hard on the nationalist press and theatres as the wartime Defence of the Realm Act took hold. When Bourke staged the play, the authorities got wind of the word and admonished the then manager, John Ervine, for allowing this 'piece of sedition' to cross the boards of the Abbey. While the offending passages may not seem out of place with many other stock speeches of the time, Levitas argues that the act of staging the play at the Abbey theatre gave it political force, elevating the melodrama beyond the limits of popular entertainment for the masses at the Queen's.[30] Bourke and his work were summarily banned from the Abbey stage, and not for the first time, Bourke ran into trouble with the authorities.[31] That said, as Morash notes, if the genre of political melodramas went without wider recognition before the Easter Rising of 1916, Bourke upped the ante by staging:

> as much Irish material as possible, drawing on a repertoire going back more than half a century. In 1919, for instance, the theatre staged only four non-Irish plays ... more than ever the Queen's was the 'Home of Irish Drama.'[32]

As the 'Home of Irish Drama,' the theatre continued the staple diet of Allen, Boucicault, Bourke, Cooke, O'Grady and Whitbread, continuing until well into the mid-1920s. By that time the 'native drama' that the Queen's had made famous was starkly incongruous with a country that had just come through the bloodiest of civil wars.[33] Their popularity waned and fizzled out, except for the 'smalls,' which played on in rural Ireland for many years afterwards. From 1928 onwards the Queen's theatre began to popularise moving pictures, as cine-variety and cinema came to absorb the entertainment marketplace.[34]

2.3   Subtle Doesn't Cut It? The Melodramatic Aesthetic

While the discussion so far has revolved around the socio-historical and political contexts informing the world of the patriotic plays, I now want to look specifically at the melodramatic form in some detail, its forms and functions and its relationship to the Irish melodramas. I do so to investigate how the form worked as popular performance on both sides of the Irish Sea, and what that might say about the operation of the form as Irish political melodrama. Understanding the melodramatic aesthetic makes plain the dramaturgies of the patriotic plays as well as informing the final discussions of melodramatic function in this chapter. To begin with, definitions are comprehensive, and Michael Booth describes the weight of the melodramatic formula as:

> ... contain[g]s every possible ingredient of popular appeal, strong emotion, of both pathetic and potentially tragic, low comedy, romantic colouring, remarkable events in an exciting and suspenseful plot, physical sensations,

sharply delineated stock characters, domestic sentiment, domestic settings, and domestic life, love, joy, suffering, morality, the reward of virtue and the punishment of vice.[35]

Some of its principal playing features came about so as to circumvent the Licensing Act of 1737 in Britain. As Booth describes, theatres that did not hold the required licence could not perform speech on stage. As a direct result, performances of melodrama amalgamated dumb show with musical accompaniment to circumnavigate the restriction as a performative means of communication for plot, character and intention to the audience. The use of music to express emotion, by means of body and facial gesture, became commonplace in the form and indicates mood and personality for stock characters. Exits and entrances as well as primary characteristics of stock stereotypes were also punctuated by melody, becoming integral to melodrama so that even when the licensing restriction no longer pertained, these ways of playing were conventionalised within the form. Booth notes that by the mid-1800s the principal melodramatic character types were broadly in place, including the "hero, heroine, villain, comic man, comic woman, good old man and good old woman."[36] Frank Rahill depicts type in much the same vein; describing stock character, "the most important of which are the suffering heroine or hero, a persecuting villain and a benevolent comic."[37] The form's dramaturgical apparatus could often incorporate twinned storylines and settings; mixing the exotic and domestic was common on Victorian melodramatic stages and spoke to the audience of both local and national concerns. So a nautical melodrama could be about glorifying "British soldiers and sailors and Britain itself"[38] while also concerning the sailor-hero's domestic life: "a loved one in a cottage ... a villainous squire with amatory designs ... [and] a ruthless landlord bent on eviction."[39] So too, as Brooks' describes, scenography had to be "expressive, and melodrama ... had most to do with transforming the traditions of stage decoration moving towards a spectacular illusionism impossible earlier."[40] Melodramatic settings could shift from gothic to pastoral to nautical or urbanised, and atmospherics were more often than not dark and foreboding to accommodate the form's eternal 'struggle' between 'good and evil.' Settings and atmospherics also represented stock characterisation so that natural disasters could be expressive of the character and also a means of dispensing with them; violent landscapes could represent the villain being 'at war with nature as well as virtue' so that, as Booth notes, various tempest-tossed landscapes were not only "indicative

[of] the upheaval of civil and natural order … but also of a potential for natural cataclysm that can usefully vanquish the villain."[41] Essential also to the melodramatic impulse is the 'strong curtain' and the use of tableaux. Indeed Brooks argues that with the tableau "more than any other single device of dramaturgy, we grasp melodrama's primordial concern to make its signs clear, unambiguous and impressive."[42] There can be several moments of truth or denouement in any one stage picture, and each of those 'curtains' is inherently dramatic representing an emotional and/or physical climax. Such moments of intensity can also be represented silently or violently in league with the visual and audio effects, culminating in the requisite power of the tableau.[43]

Both Booth and Rahill address the changing nature of the form as the Victorian age wore out with domestic melodrama becoming more urbanised, representing working class lives, emphasising social repression, legal inequality and class conflict.[44] Both also note that melodrama became as pleasurable an enjoyment for the middle classes as it moved from down market popular houses and into the theatre world at large. The assimilation of the form by the middle classes brought with it what Rahill problematically describes as a theatre of "greater sophistication and depth" so that over time, "heroines were to be discovered who were less than blameless … villains who were more to be pitied than censured … and even heroes who refused to fight."[45] Yet even as the melodramatic imagination was ghosting psychological realism on the stage, and as overt acting devices became subtler, the aesthetic of the stock character ensured that acting styles were still largely defined by the histrionic. Emotion, as Peter Brooks notes:

> was completely externalised in legible integral postures; [including the] exaggeration of facial grimace … the use of artificial diction to support a bombastic rhetoric … soliloquies were punctuated with heavy sighs and strong points were underlined by the striking the boards with ones heels.

The non-naturalistic style where the actors spoke their innermost desires to an audience assured what Brooks describes as the "legibility of signs, compounding the already expressive dramaturgy of the form."[46] The ultimate object of the melodramatic actor was, as response, to "explain [the character's] motivation on stage through carefully selected emotional reactions to the events of the play." In other words, the actor worked through a sequence of emotional responses, which could turn quickly from comedic to dramatic as unfolding events through the plot-lines, so that "the actor interpreted character and not the play; that was up to the audience."[47] Victorian melodrama was not in the business of making comment on its content, and more concerned with the totality of the physical and emotional environment in pictorial splendour, where the audience were the final arbitrators. In this way, the audience would have been very familiar with the formal thematic at work, recognising the totality of melodramatic storytelling channelled through the characters. Principal among this melodramatic patterning is the overarching idea, which Brooks terms as the "recognition and triumph of the sign of virtue … conceived to prove the existence and validity of basic moral sentiments"; this aesthetic is core to melodrama's "ethical universe".[48] However, Brooks also argues that the ethical universe works in ways particular to the form, which may channel "broader societal issues and concerns" [only] "through the *individualistic* (my emphasis) nature of the character types."[49] So and as Booth suggests, while a central thematic of the form is involved with the portrayal of contemporary societal problems, most likely (and while there are always exceptions in a theatre that encompasses such span of time and volume of works), those ills are individual to the character rather than as commentary on or overt interrogation of broader issues and societal concerns. Here the heroine or hero must battle against the forces of the villainous stereotype, yet in the world of the play, the ill does not exist outside of the character's aberrant character. Another structural essential is the nature of the power relationships portrayed on the melodramatic stage, typically those of the "squire and peasant, landlord and tenant, seducer and victim." Here again, according to Booth the representation of stock power relationships in British melodrama signifies uneasiness with broader class structures; the character of wealth and privilege is ubiquitously cast in the role of the villain, and the lower classes are victims of that oppression.[50] That said, criminality was, to middle-class Victorians, the purview of the so-called predatory or lower classes, and melodrama often reflected that dynamic. However, many melodramas situated the villain or criminality within a middle-class milieu with little or no class conflict. Whatever the relationship to the working classes; to the form's great popularity, to its text and subtexts, and to its audiences' power to decide, the general middle-class pronouncement was that melodrama for the lower orders was to be applauded for its moral certitude of virtue over vice. The edict that good must win out evil was reaffirmed again and again within the Victorian universe. And that is very useful for my purposes. For, these melodramatic ideas wrapped up in the moral world of good versus evil falls into a distinct and particular set of tensions when brought alongside the Irish political melodramas. The triumph of virtue here is largely understood as concerned with the growing nationalist politics channelled through the plays. Those mechanics of emotion,[51] which fuse the heartbeat of the form to a nationalist agenda, continue, add to and turn the discussion now.

2.4   THE 'MECHANICS OF EMOTION' IN IRISH POLITICAL MELODRAMA

In an interview for *The Irish Times* in 1893, J.W. Whitbread described well those stock character 'types' including the hero, heroine, villain and comic figure, all of whom were well established by the turn of the century in Ireland.[52] While Booth and Brooks rightly separate out the genres of melodrama and comedy, both Rahill and Booth place significance on the importance of comic stereotypes in the melodramas.[53] That said, towards the turn of the century, Irish tastes for the 'blarney and blather' of broad Irish-*themed* melodrama were on the wane, its popularity being subsumed by, as Watt suggests, the historical hero, characterising ideas of Irish bravery and self-sacrifice, enshrined in the popular imagination for a Queen's audience. Morash describes Whitbread's *Wolfe Tone* as a "typical melodramatic romantic lead, distant [and] chivalrous."[54] In similar vein, Watt essentialises the character of Henry Joy McCracken in *The Ulster Hero* as "marching to the gallows, noble, oratorical, and betrayed."[55] Moreover, for Herr, Bourke took the traditional melodramatic hero even of Whitbread's *Lord Edward* or *Sarsfield* and transformed that trope onto the local rather than the national ideal. In other words, Bourke shaped the 'worker-hero' rather than a public figure to carry the trope. In this way Herr argues that Bourke managed to transfer the characteristics of the hero, usually reserved for the aristocratic, whether symbolically or in actuality, directly onto the evolving, more realistic and more nuanced character *type* of worker-as-hero, both male and female.[56] Unsurprisingly, the stock character of the Irish heroine was often represented as being in some type of peril from nefarious characters in the plays; when encountering villains (especially those from foreign lands), women were perceived as feisty Irish maids or maidens that must be possessed sexually, or beautiful creatures to be sought after and esteemed. Interestingly, Watt makes the point that if the villain happened to be Irish, the women were often measured for their value and worth as property or estate.[57] That being said, both Watt and Fitz-Simon argue that the more political of the plays saw the women as heroine type, working across class lines, with more agency to act on their own behalf or for Ireland's cause.

Using *Wolfe Tone* as example, Fitz-Simon notes that Whitbread's dramaturgy was also adept at creating empathy with the audience by playing out the duality of, high-stakes politics with the "highly personal concerns…[of the] family unit comprised of the Tones and their faithful servants."[58] That said, Morash suggests that there is more focus on the servants than on the eponymous hero and his family, and specifically on Tone's loyal servant Shane McMahon, as "he struggles to outwit the villain-informer Rafferty."[59] Broadly, the trope of the servant typifies Watt's formulation of the comic Irishman as taking on particular stock traits, including loyalty, bravery and patriotism. The comic Irishman also has the "uncanny ability to detect plots against his aristocratic master or friend [often] affecting daring escape or rescue [which] drives the action of the play."[60] Displays of masculinity abound, as does the comic pulverising of the villain-informer with the ability to recognise the black heart of the foe before their 'patriot gentlemen' do. Watt notes that the image of the loyal Irish servant who goes about courting the 'very Irish maid' operated as a device for "conventional comic predicament and resolution," in many of the Irish political melodramas. Fitz-Simon too describes the female servants as just as loyal as the men and as patriotic and strong-minded women.[61] With that, the villain or villain-informer looms large as a significant stock character in the Irish plays. Watt makes the point that the villain-informer in many political melodramas, in addition to his nefarious and duplicitous qualities, is often portrayed as "effeminate or physically inferior"; for instance, the maid Peggy in *Wolfe Tone* is portrayed as "a wild Irish girl…[more] courageous than an effeminate adversary."[62] If justice is delayed within the plot, the villain-informer is reminded that victory will be short-lived, while Ireland's patriots will live on forever.[63] While Watt also points out that the villain became more politicised towards the turn of the century, he argues that the disparaging characterisation of the Stage Irishman by colonial hegemony had, in Irish political melodrama, come to typify the villainous stereotype. He identifies two kinds, the police informer and the hero's associate who eventually turns on him.[64] Interestingly, Watt suggests that the villain is often more tempted to turn the hero over to the colonial powers for money rather than for the love of the Crown. That said, the key character of the vile informer was always subject to the full ire of a Queen's audience who derived much teeth-gnashing pleasure from their communal hatred of the traitor and of their ultimate spectacular downfall.[65]

The aesthetics of set design and atmospherics are also marked as broadly melodramatic in the political plays. For Joseph Holloway, Whitbread's *Wolfe Tone* surpassed anything before for its "dramatic construction and stage effects," while the *Evening Herald* noted that the staging in *When Wexford Rose* (1910) was "scenic," portraying a "wonderful accuracy of setting"[66] Fitz-Simon speaks of the strong curtain at the end of *Wolfe Tone*, when he is played out (leaving for Ireland with the French) to *Vive La France! Vive l'Irlande! Vive la Liberté!*[67] The text submitted to the Lord Chamberlain (who operated as a censor in Britain) describes a powerful tableau as ending, where the villain-informer is shot on stage as Wolfe Tone declares, "So perish all traitors!"[68] Morash notes that O'Grady was a particularly strong exponent of the tableau to produce "a moment in which the actors freeze in an iconic posture at the end of a scene [or a play] to create powerfully resonant moments."[69] Watt also observes that the penchant for 'grossly sensationalistic executions' was very popular in Victorian theatre on both sides of the channel, and Bourke was strongly inclined to the tableau and the strong curtain for political and dramatic effect. In *For The Land She Loved* as end, the centre staged and martyred Betsy Grey has the flag draped over while the men kneel and pray about her body to a slowly descending curtain, is very much a case in point. Broadly too, a Queen's audience were familiar with musical scores to set the mood and atmosphere of the plays. Bourke also used the growing importance of a more politicised musical text as underscore; for *When Wexford Rose*, Bourke played *The Wearing of the Green*, a rebel song that the British had earlier banned when Boucicault had attempted to use it on stage.[70]

2.5   THE WILL OF THE GODS—AN AUDIENCE AT THE QUEEN'S

The relationship of the audience to the 'mechanics of emotion' at work in the popular plays is enshrined in the Queen's Theatre and integral to the performance event. Trotter points out that the theatre occupied a significant role in the cultural and political life of working and middle-class Dubliners. It created as Morash states "a collective identity ... which carried over from play to play,"[71] as other theatres created a temporary spectatorship for Shakespeare, Wagner or Gilbert and Sullivan. By all accounts, the Queen's encouraged active spectatorship as the popular stage resisted the rise of a more well-behaved audience; Mary Trotter infers as much when she suggests that much of the entertainment occurred in the pits and galleries. Of an audience attending Bourke's company production of *The Colleen Bawn* in 1917, the reviewer reported, "you don't need to criticise when you go to the Queen's. It's done for you by your neighbours." Joseph Holloway's account of the collaborative nature of a Queen's audience is also clear: "where patriotic sentiment was cheered and the villains hissed all over the place," pointing up the audiences' active exchange in the theatre making.[72] Trotter describes the success of the Queen's as the coming together of a number of crucial factors. The nationalist (whether imported or home grown) melodramas were popular, they were affordable across class lines, and they spoke to Irish nationalist sentiment. The Queen's encouraged lively spectatorship, while commercial success over time allowed the theatre to produce a sophisticated scenography (round towers and wolfhounds) which again spoke to stirring visions of Irish identity. Trotter argues that this 'theatrical formation' constitutive of the *popular*, the *participatory* and the *spectacular* filtered through the audience's understanding of nationalism and identity in an increasingly politicised theatre space.[73]

However, the popular houses at times offended those who represented 'authentic' Irish culture. Levitas notes that at the turn of the century, the "young pretenders to the [cultural] revival" were up against it, for the commercial theatre was a robust force, with a large and peripatetically loyal audience base.[74] The Irish Literary Theatre (ILT) was especially scornful of the commercial houses, its visions of Irish identity and even its audiences. In the ILT's manifesto of 1897, W.B. Yeats and Lady Gregory obliquely named popular drama as representing Irish identity through 'buffoonery and easy sentiment.' They held those stages responsible for perpetuating Irish men and women as 'low comic figures' or 'Stage Irishmen.' However, Ben Levitas argues that the long tradition of the 'Stage Irishman' from "degraded nemesis to sentimental hero" was developed by Dion Boucicault, making "Irish nationalism a stock virtue rather than an accusation."[75] David Krause too attributes to Boucicault the transformation from the "grotesque 'Oirish' primitive manufactured for the amusement of John Bull," [taking] "vulgar buffoonery out of the stage Irishman and made him an attractive and articulate clown who dominated the stage."[76] Nonetheless, such representations were *misrepresentations* of Ireland and its people, and the ILT meant to grow a 'literary' drama *outside* of political concerns—a theatre that could produce works in line with the best of past and present dramatic tradition.[77] Morash rightly calls into question the ILT's claim to symbolise Ireland and "Irishness," acerbically noting "Celtic and Irish dramatic literature" had long been in existence before the Irish Literary Theatre. The organisation's ability to ignore theatre history and its audiences gave the ILT a means to create one that suited their own ends and as the Abbey Theatre opened its doors for the first time in 1904, one journalist sardonically described the affair as "The Horniman-Yeats theatricals: No Low Persons Wanted."[78] With some determination, the ILT dismissed Irish theatre traditions and audiences. Refusing to see those traditions did not lessen the fact that Irish audiences were in no way unlearned in theatre, made up from different social strata and who, then as ever, were versed in:

> ... shouting down plays that offended them, and equally capable of blocking the street in front of the Queen's ... to see plays by Boucicault, Whitbread or O'Grady, which they by no means considered ... as 'misrepresentations.' In a sense, the ILT came into being by imagining an empty space where in fact there was a crowded room. (p. 117)[79]

In 1902, the *Freeman's Journal* made no bones about that pre-existing tradition:

> The ILT appealed to a limited audience because it was literary. At the other end of the Irish theatrical world we have had for many years an Irish drama that was not literary ... the Queen's Theatre—appealed very powerfully to the mind of the average man in Dublin, and especially the average working man.[80]

Although the *Freeman's Journal* was a friend to the Queen's, the he fact that the theatre was staging popular nationalist politics down the road, albeit through a different form may also have given the ILT and later the Abbey some unease.[81]

If Yeats had little time for the commercial theatre-goer, the notion for his new artistic school as 'wild and mystical' was exclusive by design, eschewing even the more acceptable theatre attendee. The Queen's had different audience concerns. In speaking of Boucicault's *The Shaughraun*, (*1874*) Morash makes the point that the play:

... performs a delicate balancing act. It opens up conflicts between ... English and Irish, landowners and peasants—and then resolves them with a melange of conventional devices. By supporting authority and resistance to authority at the same time, [it] could be all things to all audiences.[82]

Working through conventional familiarity, Boucicault's success on national and international stages depended on the form's ability to please everybody. In Ireland, Patriotic plays set in the country's bloody past, sometimes on foreign soil, for Ireland's cause, allowed them to speak to contemporary events obliquely and at a safe distance, in the full glare of the Castle and where 'God Save The King' was played at the evening's end. Plays where the balance between national and domestic concerns are reflected in its dramaturgies and where the representation of social and cultural power relationships are also clearly evident. Plays that carry the familiarity of the stereotype, of hero, heroine, villain and comic, working within the broad melodramatic formula of suspenseful if improbable plotlines and exciting situations, where emotional switches responded to each new situation. The individualisation of evil doing as resting on the aberrant nature of the villain alone and within the world of the play itself is more ambiguous in the Irish villain-informer than its British counterpart; the hooking of the stereotype to the will of the Crown complicates the trope. However the villain's working for purely mercenary or selfish ends at times, fall's broadly in line with melodramatic convention. Whatever the approach, and accepting the changing nature of Victorian styles and advancing realism in text and performance, arguably Irish acting styles also drew on the 'legible sign,' that is, the visualisation of emotion based in the "language of gesture, attitude and facial expression," so that "emotion ... was susceptible of complete externalisation ... as a visible and almost tactile entity."[83] Again, that familiarity is essential to its success for an audience; those relationships are played out as character types underneath the totality of melodramatic expression—its scenography, the atmospherics of music and stage effects, strong curtains and tableaux. Acted out against the pictorial spectacle of the plays' total physical and emotional environment that reflected back to the audience the very struggle between good and evil itself. The audience read the signs of the actor in league with its dramaturgy to create an entirety of expressive means, working in harmony with each melodramatic element functioning as part of the whole. Meaning making was the purview of the final authority: an audience, who understood that a political melodrama at the Queen's was capable of stretching the formal capacities of the melodrama to its own ends, while still living within the Boucicaultian spirit of being 'all things to all people.' Within such thinking, the shape of the form necessarily acts as overt and subvert means through which to play out nationalist and cultural concerns as Irish popular theatre, and I will return to this point a little later.

Within the staged worlds discussed here, the spirit of the comic Irishman pervades. In the popular plays he looms large; when comedy claims him, he is a character which could drive a play's action, as a 'comic catalyst' or even 'comic-rogue hero,'[84] so that the "nominal, wellborn straight hero ... a colourless figure at best, is thrown completely into the shade."[85] That being so, as Krause suggests, a kind of mirror image also exists for Irish comic women running with the myriad of 'Connlike' Stage Irishmen and as already noted by Watt including not only "peasant beauties and Anglo Irish gentlewomen" but a wide range of female roles who embodied courage, bravery and nationalist sentiment on the popular stages. The evolving sense of female representation can in Watt's view be considered as the new Stage Irishwoman, that which is "neither a shrew leading comic Irishmen by the nose or a hapless victim."[86] Increasingly the women were strong and nationalistic, so that more reductive representations of the Stage Irishwoman became unpalatable to an Irish audience. Yet, even as versions of the Stage Irishman and woman moved away from the legacy of stock imperialistic caricature,[87] broadly, that which worked for the British aesthetic also worked for the Irish version in several conventional respects. The extent to which the traditional genre stretched to house growing national sentiment as the form politicised towards the Rising of 1916, or that the dramatists became more revolutionary in their politics, does not take away from the functioning or the success of the genre. As Levitas points out more than once the 'elastic bandness' of the form's structure ultimately refuses to break; therefore, it fails to really interrogate ideas of nation and class in the patriotic plays. Such a reading would seem to take issue with the form itself, and in a sense that simplifies the conversation. To criticise the form for *being* that which it is seems redundant. There is another approach available to my way of thinking. I would like to focus the discussion not on what the form did not do; rather I would like to focus on what the form did do, in an attempt to move the conversation along. And in a way, that is what this chapter has been sketching. The melodramatic aesthetic is very close to its British neighbour, in its form and its functions, however stretched. This gave rise to anxiety in more than one quarter; for many that relationship was far too close for comfort, stigmatising the form and the works in a country moving towards self-determination, centrally concerned with creating an Irish sense of self separate from the realities of a colonised existence. That view was further complicated and copper fastened by those who believed the Queen's work and spectatorship was less than that which should constitute 'authentic' Irish drama. The stigma of cultural and political 'nearness' as the 'second city of the Empire' finally ensured that the plays became lost or hidden from view. Perhaps, to a certain degree that is why they still are. The rows and debates about their use as nationalist artefacts have been very well rehearsed, and in a sense this comes down to value judgements made on the works and their audiences, when brought alongside more established national narratives about Irish identity, theatre and war in the first decades of the twentieth century in Ireland. There are other anxieties around what constitutes art, and where popular culture fits along that spectrum, and this remains contested territory in Irish cultural discourses. Comedy too is often forced into the lesser position, finding itself relegated to divisions below or second to Ireland's dramatic worlds, and finally comedy itself can be a very difficult place for women. Under that weight Irish comic women become part of a hidden performance history here. However, acknowledging yet circumventing those discourses, while difficult gifts the work back to us in a different light. As the plays were transmitting the legible signs of nationalist, even separatist politics through the form, it's my belief that they were also transmitting *other* readable signs to their audiences by multiple means, and open to multiple interpretations. For my purpose that brings me to the comic women operating through the form and the works. Krause singles out Boucicault's women and then moves on to Synge and O'Casey to argue for a lineage of comic women in Irish drama. This leaves a gaping maw. My work intends to sit as precursor to the Widow, to Bessie Burgess, Mary Byrne and Rosie Redmond, and as successor to the comic women in Boucicault's sensations. With that in mind, the next chapter will explore the comedy at work in a selection of the patriotic plays, and the role of the female comic within those structures. In order to interrogate how the comic woman is operating, the plays are examined as exemplary of the central motifs at work, through ideas of romance, of nation and of class across the native dramas. This examination of the plays will illuminate how the comedy works and how the women work the comedy through the form. The analysis will then move forward to a detailed discussion of the permissions and constraints that women must labour within to survive and win in comic worlds, and spends some time gathering a loose association of ideas to encapsulate the comic everywoman in relationship to her audience. The last chapter connects the aesthetics discussed in these early chapters and the concepts that drive the comic everywoman, to a consideration of their practice as performance processes in Irish political melodrama.

NOTES

1. The Gaiety Theatre constituted a departure from traditional repertory theatre, which housed a resident company of performers and technicians, who staged their own productions. Instead, the Gunn brothers operated the Gaiety Theatre as a dedicated touring house, accommodating the growing number of English and American touring companies coming to Ireland as a result of new rail and steamship routes. See Christopher Morash, *A History of Irish Theatre: 1601–2000* (Cambridge: Cambridge University Press, 2002), p. 104.
2. The theatre was destroyed by fire in 1880 and was reopened in 1897, running as a touring house.
3. Joseph Holloway cited in Ben Levitas, *The Theatre of Nation: Irish Drama and Cultural Nationalism 1890–1916* (New York: Oxford University Press, 2002), p. 15.
4. Christopher Morash, *A History of Irish Theatre*, p. 106.
5. Christopher Morash, *A History of Irish Theatre*, p. 104.
6. Christopher Morash, *A History of Irish Theatre*, pp. 107–8.
7. For a more detailed discussion on touring histories, see Christopher Morash, *A History of Irish Theatre*, pp. 103–8.
8. Philip B. Ryan, *The Lost Theatres of Dublin* (Wiltshire: Badger Press, 1998), p. 64; Vikki Jackson, *Gags and Greasepaint: A Tribute to Irish Fits-Ups*, ed. by Mícheál Ó hAodha (Newcastle upon Tyne: Cambridge Scholars Publishing, 2010), p. 1.
9. The fit ups are also associated broadly with more established touring companies during the period, including Ira Allen's company, P.J. Bourke's company, Frank Delaney and H.J. Condron's company and Roberto Lena's company; by way of example, see Philip B. Ryan, *The Lost Theatres of Dublin*, p. 64.
10. Philip B. Ryan, *The Lost Theatres of Dublin*, p. 66; Christopher Morash, *A History of Irish Theatre*, p. 153.
11. Philip B. Ryan, *The Lost Theatres of Dublin*, p. 66.
12. Philip B. Ryan, *The Lost Theatres of Dublin*, p. 150.

13. For a fuller discussion on Dublin's 'Meccas of Entertainment,' see Susanne Colleary, *Performance and Identity in Irish Stand-Up Comedy: The Comic 'i'* (Hampshire: Palgrave, 2015), pp. 27–9.

14. Robert Hogan and Richard Burnham, *The Art of the Amateur 1916–1920* (Portlaoise: Dolmen Press, 1984), p. 70.

15. A cursory study of the plays performed at the Queen's from about 1912 on suggests that some such companies played more regularly than Hogan and Burnham allow.

16. *For the Land they Loved: Irish Political Melodramas 1890–1925*, ed. by Cheryl Herr, (Syracuse N.Y.: Syracuse University Press, 1991), p. 12. See also Stephen Watt, *Joyce, O'Casey and the Irish Popular Theatre* (New York: Syracuse University Press), p. 33.

17. The fact that the Queen's main rival the Theatre Royal was also closed after fire in 1880 helped position the Queen's as in de Búrca's eyes as 'The Irish National Theatre.' See Séamus de Búrca, *The Queen's Royal Theatre Dublin*, (Dublin: Séamus de Búrca, 1983), p. 1.

18. R.F. Foster, *Vivid Faces: The Revolutionary Generation in Ireland 1890–1923* (UK: Penguin Random House, 2015), p. 79. Cheryl Herr suggests that advertisements from the time support the claim for the extensive touring of the plays. *For the Land they Loved*, pp. 6–8.

19. Stephen Watt, *Joyce, O Casey and the Irish Popular Theatre*, p. 32.

20. O'Grady's first play, *The Gommach* or *The Wild Irish Boy* in 1877, was by all accounts derivative of a Boucicaultian style.

21. Of the three, *The Famine* was the only one that premiered at The Queen's in 1886; see Ben Levitas, *The Theatre of Nation*, pp. 18–19.

22. *For the Land they Loved*, p. 14.

23. Christopher Fitz-Simon, *Buffoonery and Easy Sentiment Popular Irish Plays in the Decade prior to the Opening of the Abbey Theatre* (Dublin: Carysfort Press), p. 139.

24. For a fuller discussion on Boucicault as author of *Robert Emmet*, see Deirdre McFeely, *Dion Boucicault: Irish Identity on Stage* (Cambridge: Cambridge University Press, 2012), pp. 169–192.

25. Fitz-Simon suggests that an earlier play *The Nationalist* (1891) showed signs of the more overt political overtones that became apparent in the later works; see Christopher Fitz-Simon, *Buffoonery and Easy Sentiment*, pp. 125–131.

26. *For the Land they Loved*, p. 10.

27. Christopher Morash, *A History of Irish Theatre*, p. 110.

28. Christopher Morash, *A History of Irish Theatre*, p. 153.

29. *For the Land they Loved*, p. 10.

30. Ben Levitas, *The Theatre of Nation*, pp. 220–1; see also Mary Trotter, *Ireland's National Theaters: Political Performance and the Origins of the Irish Dramatic Movement* (Syracuse N.Y.; Syracuse University Press, 2001), p. 70.

31. In 1914 the Castle pulled down the advertising posters for his play *In Dark and Evil Days*. The offending pictorials depicted a naval skirmish between the French and the British fleet in Lough Swilly in 1798; see Séamus de Búrca, *The Queen's Royal Theatre*, pp. 4–5. Bourke was also part of the early cinema world in Dublin and was heavily involved in the making of *Ireland A Nation* (1914) with Walter McNamara. When the film played at Dublin's Rotunda in January 1917, the military authorities subsequently banned its screening because a scene showing "the murder of a British soldier by a rebel was greeted with prolonged and enthusiastic applause." Interestingly, the film was re-edited in the early 1920s and married the real to the fictional. Events including footage of the burial of rebel Terence MacSwiney who died on hunger strike in Brixton connected the politics and sentiment of the patriotic plays to real-world political events, Gibbons, Hill and Rocket cited in Christopher Morash, *A History of Irish Theatre*, p. 155; Christopher Morash, *A History of Irish Theatre*, pp. 154–5.

32. Christopher Morash, *A History of Irish Theatre*, p. 154.

33. Both Cheryl Herr and Christopher Morash note that while Whitbread ran the Queen's, the theatre presented Irish material including in-house patriotic dramas, while touring shows with emphasis on Irish plays, for approximately one third of the year. See Christopher Morash, *A History of Irish Theatre*, p. 109; *For the Land they Loved*, pp.5–6.

34. For a fuller discussion of Dublin's 'Meccas of Entertainment' from the mid-1920s on, see Susanne Colleary, *Performance and Identity in Irish Stand-Up Comedy*, pp. 27–29.

35. Michael R. Booth, *Theatre in the Victorian Age* (Cambridge: Cambridge University Press, 1991) p. 151.

36. Michael R. Booth, *Theatre in the Victorian Age*, p. 153.

37. Frank Rahill, *The World of Melodrama* (Philadelphia: Pennsylvania State University Press, 1967), p. xiv.

38. Michael R. Booth, *Theatre in the Victorian Age*, pp. 152–53.

39. Michael R. Booth, *Theatre in the Victorian Age*, p. 153.

40. Peter Brooks, *The Melodramatic Imagination: Balzac, Henry James, Melodrama, and the Mode of Excess* (Yale: Yale University Press, 1995), p. 46.

41. Michael R. Booth, *Theatre in the Victorian Age*, pp. 161–2.

42. Peter Brooks, *The Melodramatic Imagination*, p. 48.

43. Michael R. Booth, *Theatre in the Victorian Age*, pp. 158–9.

44. Michael R. Booth, *Theatre in the Victorian Age*, p. 153.

45. Frank Rahill, *The World of Melodrama*, p. Xv. See also Booth's discussion on melodramatic acting and realism, Michael R. Booth, *Theatre in the Victorian Age*, pp. 129–133.

46. Peter Brooks, *The Melodramatic Imagination*, p. 47.

47. Michael R. Booth, *Theatre in the Victorian Age*, pp. 134; 39.

48. Peter Brooks, *The Melodramatic Imagination*, pp. 48–9.

49. Peter Brooks, *The Melodramatic Imagination*, pp. 48–9.

50. Michael R. Booth, *Theatre in the Victorian Age*, pp. 163–4.

51. The term is a vaudevillian one and refers to the level of pride that performers had in reading and manipulating their audiences. For a fuller discussion please see Richard Butsch, *The Making of American Audiences: From Stage to Television, 1750–1990*, (New York: Cambridge University Press, 2000), p. 95.

52. He included old man, walking gentleman and second walking gentleman as examples. If a player, whether male or female, found a particular character *type* as 'suiting' or successful with the audience, it was likely to become the actors' principal type for playing. See Séamus de Búrca, *The Queen's Royal Theatre Dublin*, pp. 18–9.

53. Booth holds off on naming the comic stereotype as essential to the functioning of the genre. He describes the melodramatic archetype as the hero, the heroine and the villain only.

54. Christopher Morash, *A History of Irish Theatre*, pp. 153–5.

55. Stephen Watt, *Joyce, O'Casey and the Irish Popular Theatre*, p. 83.

56. *For the Land they Loved*, p. 55.

57. Stephen Watt, 'Late 19th Century Irish Theatre: Before the Abbey—and beyond,' in *The Cambridge Companion to Twentieth-Century Irish Drama*, ed. by Shaun Richards (Cambridge: Cambridge University Press, 2004), p. 25.

58. Christopher Fitz-Simon, *Buffoonery and Easy Sentiment:* p. 152.

59. Christopher Morash, *A History of Irish Theatre*, p. 112.

60. Stephen Watt, 'Late 19th Century Irish Theatre, pp. 23–24.

61. Fitz-Simon is particularly referring to Anne Devlin along with the other women in Whitbread's *Insurgent Chief* (1902); see Christopher Fitz-Simon, *Buffoonery and Easy Sentiment:* p. 156; Stephen Watt, *Joyce, O'Casey and the Irish Popular Theatre*, p. 81.

62. Stephen Watt, *Joyce, O'Casey and the Irish Popular Theatre*, p. 69.

63. Stephen Watt, 'Late 19th Century Irish Theatre,' pp. 25–26. Interestingly, in the works of O'Grady as example, there exist gradations of villainy, and not necessarily informer tropes exclusively, which include scheming middle-class catholic entrepreneurs and bailiffs who carry out their bidding in plays that represented poverty and the misuse of power like *Eviction*; see Christopher Fitz-Simon, *Buffoonery and Easy Sentiment:* p. 84.

64. Watt situates the stereotype in the later plays of Boucicault and in the plays of Whitbread; his discussion centres on Boucicault's version of *Robert Emmet* and Whitbread's *The Ulster Hero*; see *Joyce, O'Casey and the Irish Popular Theatre*, pp. 78–88.

65. Christopher Morash, *A History of Irish Theatre*, p. 112.

66. *For the Land they Loved*, p. 16.

67. Christopher Fitz-Simon, *Buffoonery and Easy Sentiment:* p. 154.

68. J.W. Whitbread, 'Theobald Wolfe Tone,' in *For the Land they Loved*, pp. 171–258.

69. Christopher Morash, *A History of Irish Theatre*, p. 112

70. *For the Land they Loved*, p. 16.

71. Christopher Morash, *A History of Irish Theatre*, p. 110.

72. Joseph Holloway quoted in Christopher Fitz-Simon, *Buffoonery and Easy Sentiment*, p. 41.

73. Mary Trotter, *Ireland's National Theaters*, p. 41. Trotter also discusses the idea that the Queen's moved beyond the staging of nationalist or patriotic melodramas, an example of which were benefit nights that raised money for popular causes including the Wolfe Tone Memorial Fund (1899) and the Michael Dwyer Fund (1902). Supporting such causes allowed an audience to actively identify with broad nationalist sentiment in the early years of the twentieth century. See Mary Trotter, *Ireland's National Theaters*, pp. 59; 67.

74. Ben Levitas, *The Theatre of Nation*, p. 19.

75. Ben Levitas, *The Theatre of Nation*, p. 18.

76. David Krause, *The Profane Book of Irish Comedy* (London: Cornell University Press, 1982), p. 175.

77. Stephen Watt, 'Late 19th Century Irish Theatre,' pp. 19–20. Also, Christopher Morash, *A History of Irish Theatre*, pp. 115–117.

78. The opening night consisted of Yeats' *On Baile's Strand*; the 1798 drama, *Cathleen ni Houlihan* and Lady Gregory's *Spreading the News*; Christopher Morash, *A History of Irish Theatre*, p. 128. For a full discussion of the Irish Literary Theatre, see also pp. 115–117.

79. Morash also makes the point that ILT, not counting George Moore, had little to no interest in the theatre before they decided to form one of their own. See Christopher Morash, *A History of Irish Theatre*, pp. 115; 117. See also R.F. Foster, *Vivid Faces*, p. 79.

80. R.F. Foster, *Vivid Faces*, p. 78.

81. Perhaps too as Foster suggests, the success of *Cathleen ni Houlihan* may have in part been because of its familiarity, grounded as it was in 1798. This was nothing strange to the wealth of a Dublin audience, R.F. Foster, *Vivid Faces*, p. 79.

82. Christopher Morash, *A History of Irish Theatre*, p. 109.

83. Michael R. Booth, *Theatre in the Victorian Age*, p. 134. Peter Brooks, *The Melodramatic Imagination*, p. 46.

84. David Krause, *The Profane Book of Irish Comedy*, p. 175.
85. Frank Rahill, *The World of Melodrama*, p. 190.
86. Stephen Watt, *Joyce, O'Casey and the Irish Popular Theatre*, p. 70. Also, see 'Late 19th Century Irish Theatre,' p. 27.
87. Mary Trotter, *Ireland's National Theaters*, pp. 71–2.

Bibliography

Booth, Michael R. 1991. *Theatre in the Victorian Age*. Cambridge: Cambridge University Press.

Brooks, Peter. 1995. *The Melodramatic Imagination: Balzac, Henry James, Melodrama, and the Mode of Excess*. Yale: Yale University Press.

Colleary, Susanne. 2015. *Performance and Identity in Irish Stand-Up Comedy: The Comic 'i'*. Hampshire: Palgrave.

de Búrca, Séamus. 1983. *The Queen's Royal Theatre Dublin 1829–1969*. Dublin: Séamus de Búrca.

Fitz-Simon, Christopher. 2011. *Buffoonery and Easy Sentiment: Popular Irish Plays in the Decade Prior to the Opening of the Abbey Theatre*. Dublin: Carysfort Press.

For the Land They Loved: Irish Political Melodramas 1890–1925, ed. Cheryl Herr (Syracuse: Syracuse University Press, 1991).

Foster, R.F. 2015. *Vivid Faces: The Revolutionary Generation in the 1890–1923*. UK: Penguin Random House.

Hogan, Robert, and Richard Burnham. 1984. *The Art of the Amateur 1916–1920*. Portlaoise: Dolmen Press.

Jackson, Vikki, 2010. *Gags and Greasepaint: A Tribute to Irish Fits-Ups*, ed. Mícheál Ó hAodha. Newcastle upon Tyne: Cambridge Scholars Publishing.

Krause, David. 1982. *The Profane Book of Irish Comedy*. London: Cornell University Press.

Levitas, Ben. 2002. *The Theatre of Nation: Irish Drama and Cultural Nationalism 1890–1916*. New York: Oxford University Press.

McFeely, Deirdre. 2012. *Dion Boucicault: Irish Identity on Stage*. Cambridge: Cambridge University Press.

Morash, Christopher. 2002. *A History of Irish Theatre, 1601–2000*. Cambridge: Cambridge University Press.

Rahill, Frank. 1967. *The World of Melodrama*. Philadelphia: Pennsylvania State University Press.

Ryan, Philip B. 1998. *The Lost Theatres of Dublin*. Wiltshire: Badger Press.

Trotter, Mary. 2001. *Ireland's National Theaters: Political Performance and the Origins of the Irish Dramatic Movement*. Syracuse: Syracuse University Press.

Watt, Stephen. 1991. *Joyce, O'Casey and the Irish Popular Theatre*. New York: Syracuse University Press.

———. 2004. Late 19th Century Irish Theatre: Before the Abbey—And Beyond. In *The Cambridge Companion to Twentieth-Century Irish Drama*, ed. Shaun Richards. Cambridge: Cambridge University Press.

CHAPTER 3

Comic Texts

Abstract This chapter makes a series of in-depth comic analyses from a selection of the patriotic plays under the recurring themes of romance, nation and class. The plots are briefly described as a way into the comic structures operating in the plays, its mechanics and its intentions interwoven through the central motifs. The analysis draws out the device of the comedy double act along its porous edges to understand how the women operated in and out of the doubling. It discusses the plays' usage of satirical attack, light relief and comic violence or slapstick. The chapter reveals the scope of comic expression in the plays and makes plain the levels of comic female agency working through the central motifs.

Keywords Romance • Nation • Class • Courtship • Satire • Violence • Comedy

3.1   The Comedy of Romance, Nation and Class

From studying a selection of the patriotic plays thematically and from practice work with the scripts, I discovered that there were central and recurring motifs working across the play structures. Those motifs I broadly outlined as romance, nation and class, which are layered onto conventional melodramatic structures in the selected patriotic plays. To understand the works was to make plain those recurring motifs. So doing acted as a

S. Colleary, *The Comic Everywoman in Irish Popular Theatre*,
Palgrave Studies in Comedy,
https://doi.org/10.1007/978-3-030-02008-8_3

lens through which to focus in on the comedy in the plays, how the comedy worked, its intents and purposes as interwoven through those motifs. As one means of approach to this study, navigating the patterns of romance, nation and class reveals comic structure and purpose through the large, formulaic and convoluted plays. Importantly, this approach also began to reveal the mechanics and functionality for the comic women operating in the works. This chapter charts those series of investigations, to explore the ways in which the comedy operates and to what end within the larger score of the political melodramas. A number of discoveries were made. The chapter speaks to the comic formal expression of the double act and to the agenda of the satirist. It speaks to the plays' usage of light relief and comic violence or slapstick. It also makes consideration of comic female agency, sexual violence and dangerous women. I use these terms here in a general sense as they appear frequently in the comic analyses. The next chapter gathers up these generalities and applies them to the comic thinking of their usage in order to deepen the discussion and to focus in depth on the women who are making the comedy. I have selected a number of scenes from a selection of the plays, all taken from Cheryl Herr's excellent work as source material and all of which were revived frequently, or popular at the Queen's Theatre into the 1920s. These plays are exemplary of the evolving form and their comic function. I do so to represent how the motifs work closely together, with each play utilising the patterns to their own ends, and to key into the comic bloodline flowing through them. The next sections of the work then take for their material four patriotic plays based in the 1798 rebellion for comic analysis, J.W. Whitbread's *Lord Edward or 98* (1894), and *Wolfe Tone* (1898), P.L. Bourke's *When Wexford Rose* (1910) and *For The Land She Loved* (1915). The plots are briefly described within the scene work with the comic structures and comic women drawn out and discussed.

3.2   Comic Works—*Lord Edward* or *98* (1894)

The seeds of a romantic relationship ignite between Lord Edward's servant, Thady McGrath, "a boy of the right sort, true to the core" (83), and Kitty Malone, a servant in Pamela's (Lord Edward's love interest) household. In the first scene, Thady spies Kitty as she enters the salon in Madame De Seillery's house in Paris. He thinks her a beauty and approaches her. Their initial interchange sees Thady's failing attempts to flirt with Kitty, who as she seems only to speak French 'misconstrues' his intentions, and the comedy of misunderstanding is created for the audience. When Kitty teases Thady about not understanding her, "Oui, Oui, You no understand. You (*poking him in the ribs*) English," Thady is quick to a stung retort, "Bedad I'm not, I'm true Irish," (94). It soon becomes apparent, however, that Kitty is making a fool of Thady, revealing that she herself is Irish "and as good Wicklow born an' bred as yersilf, me bhoy" (95). Once Thady realises that Kitty is 'no Frenchman,' he immediately attempts to get a kiss "for the sake ov the ould country." The scene moves back and forth between identity and romance, as Kitty eludes Thady's advances, with feisty fighting talk, "Ye're an impudent bosthoon," before finally allowing him to court her, "yer breath is like a whiff of air from off the top ov the Wicklow Mountains." They soon discover they are related in the old country, which seals their romance. Thady remembers how she mistreated him when they were children: "do you remember now ... the polthogues (slaps) you used to trate me to on this snout?" (96), which brings a sort of violent comic nostalgia to the scene. When Lord Edward enters the scene with Pamela, Thady speaks freely, courting an embarrassed Kitty who tries to extract herself from his arms. While Lord Edward rebukes Thady for 'forgetting' himself, Thady replies, [of courting], "if it's good enough for his lordship, sure it's good enough for the likes ov me" (97). Indeed, Pamela and Lord Edward soon marry although Pamela has other suitors who desire her and the threat of sexual violence towards her is evident on occasion in the work. That said, Thady and Kitty work within a comedy doubling in large part, and at times, the comic weight of the scenes can fall to Thady rather than Kitty who acts as a foil or straight man to his comedic strides. While the theme of Irish identity is apparent and carries slapstick nostalgia, it is the comedy of courtship and the collapse of class boundaries that create the comedy here.

In act two, scene one, Thady and Kitty are with Lord Edward and Pamela in the family seat in Dublin, where Lord Edward is in imminent danger of arrest as a rebel. Thady and Tony (another servant who is a black man and the subject of racist humour) are guarding Lord Edward while he rests in his chamber. Thady and Kitty's courtship continues with misunderstanding as comic device. Not knowing Thady is nearby, Kitty speaks 'ill' of him; "love him, that spalpeen, a man that was born to die wid a hempen rope around his neck; such riff raff as that is not good enough to be my husband"(107). Thady finds her out and neither temper improves. A verbal 'sparring' match ensues, with each flinging insult onto injury:

Kitty: I'm thinkin' there's a pig in the room
Thady: Lave it then, and it'll be gone …
Kitty: An' did I give up Paris, an' the fine brave lookin' men over there
         for the likes ov yez?
Thady: … Ye jumped at me
Kitty: Well, it's sorry I am now, at any rate
Thady: So am I … Go back! Go back, to yer frog-eatin' onion growin',
         dirthy wine drinkin' Parlez-vooers; ye're not good enough for a
         dacent Irishman. (108–9)

This pseudo-satirical cut and thrust are integral to the servants' courting rituals in the patriotic melodramas and were very familiar to a popular audience. That said, the scene switches quickly to national concerns as soldiers of the Crown come to arrest Lord Edward. Kitty screams, "Oh! I will be kilt," to which Thady jabs, "No such luck"; thereafter, the scene moves to Thady saving his master from arrest with help from Kitty. Thady makes fun of the British officer Major Swan, "ye are becoming quite at home visiting her ladyship so often ….. oh, stay a little longer, we'll ord-her dinner for yez" (109–110). Interestingly, Kitty's lines are open to interpretation when she suggests, "maybe [Swan] would like to search me," to which Thady replies, "I'd like to catch him at it" (109). That said, it is the two in accord that help rescue Lord Edward from a prison cell, and time and again in these plays, we see the servants saving their masters with and without each other. The comedy of misunderstanding along with the idea of the servants as orchestraters of their masters' res-cue (usually from the British forces) drives the comedy in the work. At times Kitty has some agency outside the doubling. Act two, scene three is set on a mountain pass near Dublin. The United Irishmen are readying themselves for battle with the King's forces, as Kitty manages to slip into the camp unnoticed. She disguises herself in men's clothing and con-fronts Thady with a gun "move a slip, an' ye're a live corpse." Thady overcomes her, and she shouts "Oh, don't shoot me, sure I'm only a woman, sure I only wanted to give ye a bit ov a fright." When asked by Lord Edward what the matter is, Thady replies, "only Kitty playin' at sodgerin' yer honour" (124–25). The comedy here is tied to the idea of women 'playing at sodgerin', although the fact that it is attempted gives her a moment of satirical agency, so the vignette is a double-edged comic sword and its playing is open to interpretation by the audience. The scene also functions as a lighter moment to the drama of warfare playing out through this scene. That said as the play moves on, the servant duo continue to save their masters, interspersed with feisty love talk and humorous interchanges.

Lord Edward is at times cut with large action scenes between the Crown or enemy and the servants with their masters, where comic violence happens and pain is inflicted on either side. In act three, scene three, Kitty, who is acting outside the double, attempts to get a letter to Lord Edward warning him of imminent (once again) danger. The Crown's forces soon set upon her. A struggle ensues as Kitty resists Major Sirr and his soldiers. They attempt to rifle her and she throws them off defiantly. She mocks the soldiers, promising violent repercussion; "search me, will ye, ye dirthy ould lobster, not if I know it, come a step closer if ye dare, an' I'll give yer a taste ov me ten virgins" (143). Major Sirr becomes enraged with her and speaks with 'savage' tones, which implies a sexual subtext. She gets free of the men holding her, but is recaptured by the Major, 'turning' her around to his men again. She calls for Thady, to which Sirr responds "But Thady isn't here to help you" (144), highlighting the vulnerability of her position as a woman in peril for the audience. Thady suddenly appears, knocking soldiers, one on top of the other to the ground. He saves a gladiatorial Kitty, and they attempt to make their escape. Sirr and the soldiers hold them at the point of a bayonet; Thady throws Sirr off, who in turn fires at Thady, when Lord Edward appears to stop the action. Large fight scenes with enemy forces, where threatened or actual comic violence occurs and which also contains the threat of sexual violence, were common to the dramaturgy. The comic duo work both in and out of the doubling and are about saving their masters. Kitty is actively involved in fighting off her enemies although saving the threat to her safety and virtue reverts to Thady. The servants and the rebels, as winning, outsmarting or stalling the English forces also works for the comedy, and for a popular audience.

In act four, scene one, once again comic misunderstanding is at play as Thady tries to avert some British soldiers from finding Lord Edward's hiding place. When asked by Major Swan why he is loitering in that area, Thady invents a wife and ten children nearby in Puddin' lane. Kitty enters on the scene and becomes caught up in Thady's lie, which for a moment she believes to be true, "oh, yer villain yer, an' ye tell me that, me (*goes up to him*) that ye've been courting." However, she soon realises the ruse and joins in:

Kitty:	What is she like? Does she squint?
Thady:	Wid both eyes
Kitty:	An' has she a wooden leg?
Thady:	She has, two ov them.
Kitty:	I'll tell her, an' if it wasn't for her and the childher, I wish they'd hang yez twice over. (147–48)

The comedy duo here, with both characters more or less carrying equal weight (although again the scene ultimately belongs to Thady), works under the satirical sign, where Kitty as antagonist makes some blistering attacks on Thady, even when the ruse is known to her. The style of attack mirrors those between the two earlier, with this and the subsequent scene work providing lighter comic moments by the duo for the audience in advance of the darker drama unfolding. Within a relatively short time, Lord Edward is shot, stabbed and captured by the Crown. The comic impulse speaks as before, to the idea that Thady and Kitty are again about saving their masters, getting the better of enemy forces and repeating that enjoyment for the audience. Interestingly while Lord Edward marries Pamela early in the play, Whitbread holds Thady and Kitty's proposal scene until near its end, when Thady applies, "if we wait any longer we'll both be too ould entoirely for marriage felicity altogether" (157). The proposal can also be read as a lighter moment before the tragic death of Lord Edward from his wounds in Newgate Gaol and it's clear that here at the end, there is no comic resolution to be found.

3.3   Comic Works—*Wolfe Tone* (1898)

In Whitbread's other major history play *Wolfe Tone*, the same motifs can be seen at work. Again the comedy of the courting couple is threaded throughout the four-act play, this time by Peggy Ryan, a maid of Susan Witherington, soon to be Mrs Tone, and Shane McMahon, a college porter for Trinity College Dublin. Shane is our 'boy of the right sort' here and a loyal patriot. He makes clear his admiration for the "purty colleen" when she enters with a note for Mr Tone from her mistress. Shane assumes wrongly that it is Peggy who wishes to see Mr Tone who is "a divil wid the petticoats" (175). Peggy hears Shane whispering to Russell (a friend of Wolfe Tone) about her, and taking offence, insult follows injury:

Peggy: … always clean yer tongue when ye address a lady … you're here to wait on yer shupariors. Be off wid ye, an' when ye bring me back the answer, I'll give ye a copper penny for yez throuble.

Shane: ye can kape yer copper penny … I wouldn't [d]emane myself to touch it. (177)

Not unlike Kitty and Thady, comic misunderstanding drives their initial biting interchanges, yet Peggy and Shane soon soften their stances towards one another. Peggy suggests to Wolfe Tone (who has entered the scene) that he elope with her mistress, "Yes, do it! An' I'll help ye. Sure the darlin'[s] dying ov luv for ye." To Tone's worry about her taking such a radical step, Peggy replies, "Will she consint: Arrah! Will a kitten lap cream? What a gom ye are, Sir to aix such a question" (182). Immediately Peggy and Shane come to the aid of Wolfe Tone who has no financial means to marry, "I am the poorest wretch in Dublin this minute" (182). Both servants give their savings hidden in their socks to Wolfe Tone to aid the marriage. Wolfe Tone's wedding to Susan is carried off through a convoluted plot and embroiling all including Wolfe Tone's enemies who do not wish to see the marriage take place. Peggy and Shane continue courting and fighting throughout, "give us a kiss … didn't ye want it?" to which Peggy responds, "it's a mulvatherin villain so ye are; an' ye've no manners at all." Shane puts the come thither on her, "well come here girl & tache me better" (195). However, Shane soon switches to patriotic mode, turning again to saving Wolfe Tone who, now married, is about to be arrested for debt by the lawyer and villain-informer (who is in the pay of the castle) Rafferty. Shane pays the debt and kicks Rafferty, who falls flat on his face to the ground. The motifs of romance and class and, perhaps to a lesser extent, nation are very apparent in these first scenes. There is mirroring of high and lower orders love, with the servants conventionally carrying the comic weight. Peggy's agency is also clear, and the comedy lies in her collapsing of class boundaries with Wolfe Tone. Both she and Shane also save their masters by removing financial obstacles to the marriage and the honeymoon; as with Thady and Kitty in *Lord Edward*, their *knowing* better and being able to solve those obstacles bring the comedy in the scenes. That said, Shane carries more of the comic power towards the end, and in flattening Rafferty, he also creates some slapstick comic action along class and nationalist lines to close in the first act.

Act two is set seven years later, Tone and Susan are married with three children, and like Kitty and Thady before them, Shane and Peggy have not yet made it up the aisle. Shane bemoans the fact: "if Peggy there had only been sensible we might have been married an' had three [children], too" (201). Peggy gives short shrift, and the conversation moves on. When Tone arrives with guests for dinner, Shane asks Peggy, "Any money in the house?" to which she replies, "not a shillin, and the credit's gone entoirely." Shane gives money to Peggy to get "all ye want & say nuthin" (203) and also produces whiskey, as the house is dry. Shane and Peggy's covering for Tone's poverty saves the masters from social embarrassment, and as before, the irony of the situation is plain to an audience. From this point in the second act, the action switches very clearly to the cause for Ireland's freedom although the themes of romance and betrayal maintain. Accusations of Mrs Tone's adultery by Samuel Turner, the United Irishman, and (another) informer turn the storyline. Rejected in love by Susan Tone, he seeks to harm both, through the convoluted plot as stock melodrama. Sullying Mrs Tone's reputation results in a skirmish. Peggy knocks Rafferty to the ground and stands over him with a chair, while Shane, on entering throws Turner to the ground. The scene exacts comic violence and pain as the servants attempt to save Tone, forming a tableau to end. In-house fighting and wrangling among the United Irishmen carry the second act in typical melodramatic fashion, with Wolfe Tone chosen to depart for France to solicit aid for Ireland's cause. Interestingly, Shane makes reference to a British Officer as not being a 'bad lot' even as he wears the Red Coat of the enemy; the sentiment is also echoed in *Lord Edward*, and speaks to the melodramatic convention of emphasising individual vices and virtues rather than to broader societal good or ill. That being said, the comedy in the action scenes is wrought through enjoyment of the enemy's comeuppance through comic violence.

Act three is set in a French encampment where Tone has finally managed to convince the French to consider dispatch of another army to Ireland. Where Tone is, Shane is soon to follow, married now and with newborn twins. Peggy and Mrs Tone arrive from Paris and are reunited with their husbands. Peggy and Shane banter, she thinks him fine in his 'jerrymintals' and extols that "it will be a grand thing to be … the widdy ov a hayro." Shane is not happy, muttering, "Am I worth more to yez did than livin?" They talk of their newborn son, "thrue Leinster ivery inch ov him," to which Shane replies, "on both sides?" (225). The comment seems to reflect his jealousy, with a less than subtle accusation that Peggy might have been unfaithful and is in hopeful anticipation of his demise. Again the antagonistic sparring between them brings the comedy, and Peggy's ambivalence as a way of playing adds to the layered comedic value of the moment. The flow moves swiftly to Napoleon Bonaparte's entrance with Tone arranging to meet the General to discuss France's aid to Ireland. Equally both Shane and Peggy have no compunction in speaking their mind to both Napoleon and Josephine, his wife; and again the comedy of collapsing class lines underpins the scene. A little later, Josephine arrives to talk to Susan of their husbands' meeting. An attempt is made to kidnap Susan by Hans who is in the pay of the villain Turner. Turner (still) seeks revenge for Susan's rejection of him. Hans' instruction is to put Susan Tone on a ship for South America to be sold to a Brazilian farmer. He is bested by the women with Peggy, letting fly several times at the Dutchman, "Ye've got yer ordher, yer dirthy Dutch haddock (*flourishes broom*). Go! Or I'll spifflicate yez"(236). She hits him out the door with the broom. However, Turner returns with Rafferty, Hans and other ruffians to complete the mission. Peggy attempts to "choke the dirthy life out ov yez," grabbing Rafferty before she is manhandled by the others; on seeing Hans, she flings fighting talk at the "dirthy lump ov mouldy Dutch cheese," but she is overcome by her assailants. Hans gags her and threatens with "Yah, I sall cut your claws for you when I gets you mit myself on board mine sheep." Others tie her hands and legs to a chair. Turner promises Susan a similar fate, "In an hour you will be on board that man's ship (points to Hans) bound for South America. When you arrive you will be disposed of—Sold—to a man half nigger-half Spaniard … he is waiting to receive you with open arms" (238–9). The threats of assault and rape are clear, and Peggy's confrontational defiance, whilst satirical and comic, is tinged with the thrill of tension and danger. The resolution comes in the form of Shane who, disguised and under the table, frees Peggy's bonds where she has been tied, and both threaten comic violence and pain with a poker and a pistol. Brandishing the poker Peggy cries "stir a step and I'll brain yez!" (240). The scene ends in tableau with Tone, who has been trying to enter for some time still shouting, "Let me in!" (240). Once again Peggy, who has strong agency in the scene, and Shane save their masters with Tone left to bang on the door outside. The comedy works here through Peggy's defiance and her comic violence even as she and her mistress are in danger of kidnap, assault and forced marriage in a foreign land. The threat of sexual assault is clear; Peggy's fight wins the first round; however, it takes Shane to save the day, so her comic agency is mediated by his actions. That said, in the end both are the architects of victory in aid of their betters and in defeat of the foe. As with *Lord Edward*, the idea of rescued virtue works alongside Saving the masters here and with the enemy's defeat in Ireland's cause. The relationship sets up a complicated, but not an unfamiliar, structure in the plays where nation as pattern is inscribed onto the embodied and imperilled woman.

As the play moves through the third and into its final act, Shane and Peggy meet once more with the traitors that are attempting to thwart Wolfe Tone at every turn. Peggy does attack Rafferty again, with comic effect, calling him "ya scum of Dhublin Castle ye!" (243). Both Peggy and Shane attempt to save their masters again to varying degrees of failure and success, and with more or less equal comic weight, which could suggest light relief for the audience, although the overall tone of Wolfe Tone is more hopeful than other works under discussion. As the play moves to a more serious mode for the final scenes, Peggy and Shane not unlike Kitty and Thady before them move into the background. Rafferty and Turner are discovered as villain-informers, and Rafferty is executed centre stage. Wolfe Tone leaves for the war in Ireland, and Whitbread does not overtly allude to the reality of the rebellion's end in 1798 or to the brutality of Wolfe Tone's death by his own hand in an Irish gaol. The theme for Whitbread's *Wolfe Tone* is one of hope for Ireland and engaged the audience with a large degree of suspension of disbelief and wish fulfilment rather than the need for historical accuracy.

3.4   Comic Works—*When Wexford Rose* (1910)

P.J. Bourke's first major work, *When Wexford Rose* (*WWR*), is a four-act melodrama cast somewhat in the mould of what had come before while contrasting that theatrical history in certain respects.[1] *WWR* is built on a succinct first act, comprising of two short scenes, structurally this does differ from Whitbread's work, while the play itself is also a shorter consideration. That said, the principal motifs for transmission to a Queen's audience are evident within the more economic structure, and a number of relationships are quickly made apparent. Ned Traynor, a servant of the manor, is our 'boy of the right sort' here. Kitty Cassidy is not given any description other than 'in love with Ned,' but it becomes clear that she too is a servant of the Bassett estate in Wexford. Of that house, Grace Bassett is described as a young Wexford lady in love with Donal O'Byrne, our hero, described as a "young Wexford Gentleman in the service of France" (261). Grace however, is the object of Colonel Needham's (commander of the ancient Britons) affections who has taken advantage of her uncle, Captain Hoursley's (of the Wexford Yeomanry), gambling habits to gain Grace's hand in marriage. Meanwhile the Wicklow and Wexford insurgents are plotting and carrying out rebellious acts through the local countryside. With the 1798 rebellion as backdrop, Bourke introduces the romantic apparatus of melodrama. Grace is in love with Donal, and as 'high' to 'low' mirror, Kitty is in love with Ned. The servants' romantic relationship is established quickly, and their 'courtin' is of those already in love. When he woos her with compliments, Kitty cuts him short with "don't be making a fool of yourself, isn't the whole country disturbed enough without his Riverence catchin' us like this." Ned responds, "lave it to me to watch that, and as for makin' a fool of me self I'd do more than that for you Kitty darlin." Their soft banter and playfulness very soon gives way to talk of what's to come:

Ned: I want to talk what you call foolish. It may be a long time before we stand here together again, & I want to know will you have what's left of me when the war is over.

Kitty: Did you ever doubt me, Ned? (*Kiss*) (268)

This gentle comedy of courtship is in a sense short-circuited by the fact that Kitty and Ned as well as Grace and Donal's relationships are already established from the outset, differing from the melodramatic structures already discussed. The succinctness of the first act necessitates that economy while Bourke's own political aesthetics may also have had a bearing. It feels as if this structure is intent on getting to the heart of the political matter with perhaps not as much emphasis on the more convoluted and comic melodramatic conventions. That being said, Kitty and Ned's comedy of courting is familiar, episodic and short-lived. These lighter moments between the couple quickly turn to a more serious tone when Ned seeks assurance that Kitty will still love him if he is injured in the fighting. The rebellion feels real and close, and Kitty makes no joke about being the "widdy of a hayro" as Peggy did before her, for the atmospherics are sobering and achieved at a 'fair clip' in this play. Those atmospherics are also aided by the presence of Biddy Dolan and in certain respects the scenes between Ned and Biddy work as inverse to Ned and Kitty as the established courting couple and comedy double . Biddy Dolan is described as a 'notorious informer' and, not unlike Lady Rose in Whitbread's *Sarsfield*, is cast, for a woman, in the unusual role as the villain-informer. Described by Ned to Donal as:

... arm in arm with the Government in Wexford ... there isn't a woman or child about the neighbourhood that not in dread of their lives of her ... sure only she's a woman she'd be shot long ago. (265)

Biddy Dolan is an object of fear for the community and in the pay of Needham to ensure Grace does not marry the hero-rebel Donal O'Byrne. When Ned encounters Biddy towards the end of the first act, she is scouting for information:

Biddy: On my way up I saw a strange gentleman ... I don't remember seeing him before in these parts
Ned: Maybe it's the [new] Docthor ... I am—very sick
Biddy: You, Ned? There's not a feather out of you
Ned: Bedad & I'm sick all the same. I' m sick of people tryin' to get news out of me ... so you can try your hand at getting information somewhere else
Biddy: I think Ned, you are carrying the joke too far. (269)

Ned's satire is aggressive and defiant towards Biddy who is fact-finding for Needham. He has no intention of telling her anything of Donal, and in response Biddy has little compunction in threatening Ned, making plain her dangerous power, and the darker comedy works to incite the pleasure of hatred for the popular audience.

Needham's relationship with the 'informer' also works comedically and in some unexpected ways. Near the beginning of act two, Biddy mocks Needham for his stupidity at being bested by the rebels. Needham threatens to "settle with O'Byrne" yet. Biddy replies:

Not in single combat, O Byrne is too swift and sure with [his] sword for your sort ... a coward who would not meet any man face to face. Why, I should not fear to meet you and cross swords with you myself. (272)

While Biddy mocks Needham, the comedy generated is based on two despised characters (perhaps one more despised than the other) at odds with one another. Such odds create that sense of enjoyable hatred of both characters for the audience. To add to that, there is also a sense that an audience at the Queen's would have found pleasure in Biddy's ridicule of Needham for its own sake; as an instrument of the Crown, the audience must have enjoyed Biddy's biting insult of Needham's prowess. The satirical edge sharpens in differing directions when Biddy and Needham accost Kitty and Mary Doyle, who is known as the 'heroine of Ross.' He insults them as "Rebel Hussies," and Mary responds with "At your service, Colonel" (*Bows mockingly*), while Kitty taunts them with false cordiality. Needham immediately threatens violence, to which Kitty responds with "Did anyone ever hear such cheek from a blind ould lobster like that?" Mary soon changes the tone and tells Needham to go to "the Devil, with yourself and your King" and also threatens to do violence, and when they exit, Kitty states, "the sight of that pair was making me sick" (274). Kitty and Mary's mocking tones in the face of dark power are tinged with danger, and the scene demonstrates the knife-edge between the satirical impulse at work and the threat of more realistic violence in the play. On one level that propensity in the play to 'turn on a sixpence' between mockery and violence feels immediate; this may be to do with Bourke's stylistic of injecting elements into the melodramatic form where realism and comedy are drawn very closely together. Interestingly, the figure of Grace Bassett is locked out of the early agency that Kitty and Mary own, and her role is much more passive initially. Earlier in the play when Grace is envious of the men who will be in the thick of the battle, Donal responds by suggesting that Grace "shall find work to do in a sphere of action more suited to your strength ... in the fight for life and home the women of Ireland must aid their struggling brothers in every way" (268). In these early stages Grace can only fulfil a secondary role unlike her sisters in war. It's possible that the character is restrained by some structure of the heroine, so that she seems to have little access to the agency, risk and language of mockery that the other women possess. However, that does change as the play progresses, which marks a development of the character, again somewhat unusual in stock formation. As the act moves forward, Kitty and Ned continue their soft banter as he woos her, while Kitty's power as a wilful and feisty woman pertains. Again, the comedy works in these scenes through comic courtship, Kitty's agency and the women's satirical bite in the face of the enemy; all of which lighten the immediacy of war in this play.

At the top of act three, the rebel women are praised for their fighting on the front line. Ned speaks to Kitty after the battle for New Ross has taken place, "I'd go without tay for the rest of me days to see you and Mary Doyle fightin' the yeos. Faith I won't forget New Ross as long as I live. It's many a life the pair of you saved & Master Donal himself wouldn't be here only for your bravery" (284). The tales of the women's deeds indicate their active roles in the rebellion, and the war stories permeate these scenes in relationship to the comic tones. Kitty enters with guns and ammunition, and when Ned asks her if she took them from the enemy, she responds with "faith they threw them away so as they could run aisy" (285). Unlike Whitbread's concessions to individual merit, Kitty's comedy of mockery, towards the British soldiers, tars all with the same brush; Bourke does not account for those allowances in his works. Her comic disdain is also signalled through Mary, yet on the whole Mary mantles the heroic role of an Irish woman as soldier. Meanwhile, Grace tries to help an old widow under threat from the King's soldiers and in melodramatic style; Colonel Foote takes a liking to her, "Ha There's a pretty wench. Then you come with me" (288). He throws the widow off making for Grace and they struggle; however, Mary Doyle comes to her aid, throwing him off and killing Colonel Foote, while stealing his war dispatches in the process. There is more than a sense here that the rebel women are about saving their masters, whether the gentleman Donal O'Byrne on the battle-field or Grace Bassett in her attempts to help the widow woman. While the war stories of their deeds have been recounted rather than witnessed, here the comic violence and pain take place centre stage. Mary rescues Grace (who has given some fight) from a dubious and perhaps violent fate; the pleasure is wrought in the enemy's comeuppance by an Irishwoman soldier, and in the act of her stealing the dispatches to save the rebellion. There is also the signal to the saving of Grace's virtue, again hooking the symbology of nation to the embodied and imperilled woman in these plays. That said, it is clear that Grace is moving into a more active role and as mentioned earlier, that development is somewhat at odds for stock. Overall, these comic action scenes are comparatively shorter than the plays that went before which does mute the extent of comic effect for the audience. Again they feel short-circuited from a Whitbreadian style in that they quickly pattern reversion to the visceral immediacy of the struggle for independence. Bourke's stylistic clearly speaks to his overt political aims for the playwork.

In act three, scene two, Biddy's relationship with Needham darkens. She tells him (Needham is still trying to gain Grace Bassett in formulaic style) that she knows O'Byrne is hiding at the Old Mill in Carnew. When asked by Needham to kill him, Biddy replies:

Biddy: Surely, Colonel; you don't want me to win honour for you to
            wear. We can do the jobs ourselves [together]
Needham: Would you entrap me?
Biddy: Only in the same cage as myself

Needham: You proceed to the mill and await me there. This time it shall
            be a case of "Walk into my parlour," says the spider to the fly
            (*Exit*)
Biddy: Take care Colonel, that you don't be the fly. But where he
            fails to catch the rebels, I'll make sure I get my money all the
            same (291)

The exchange clearly illustrates Biddy's cunning when dealing with
Needham and raises pleasurable bile in the audience. While both characters are traced through the whole of the play as that of a despicable union,
and even as Biddy's satirical jousting with him is enjoyable for the audience, the real pleasure is in loathsome Biddy. Loyal to no one, playing with
a rebel's life, bargaining over the price with no regard for nation or man,
Biddy is grotesquely satisfying for an audience. As the play progresses,
Ned and Donal are at the old mill in Carnew, where Ned who knows better, is advising Donal how best to escape if soldiers should come. Their talk
of tradition and memory is both pleasantly light-hearted and poignant.
Ned leaves, and Mary Doyle enters, as do the British soldiers. Biddy shoots
and then drowns Mary Doyle by "pitching her into the mill race [to] finish
her" (298). Grace (who is also and improbably at the mill) tries to stop the
act and again is accosted by Needham who threatens her with death and
orders her to "remain here with me till I can get a clergyman to marry us"
(298). She resists, preferring death to marriage. Needham orders his men
to capture her while he seizes her; she screams and shoots a sergeant as the
entrance of Donal, Ned and his men overpower their struggle. The scene
ends in tableau. The comic structures work through Ned's knowingness
of the place, his loyalty to his master and their banter, acting as momen-
tary light relief to that which follows. Needham's attempted assault on
Grace and the threat of forced marriage enacts the comic violence in the
scene and again Grace's virtue is tied to the acts of the coloniser, although
here she resists with the agency of full force. Meanwhile Biddy's actions in
Mary's death are designed to excite the very last drop of gratifying rage for
the audience. As the play moves into its final act Biddy extracts money
from a reluctant Needham for her 'services' in bringing patriots to the
hangman's rope, and does so in as cruel a fashion as an audience could
enjoyably stand. She informs Needham of the French army's arrival in
Mayo, which dismays the Colonel, who is in no mood for fighting the
French. Meanwhile Grace is getting ready to wed Donal and Ned and
Kitty briefly court here, with Kitty's hoping that "the Frinch sogers [will]

... larrup the mischief out of the murderin red coats" (304). The vignette brings light relief, before Donal must leave for France to aid Wolfe Tone and push for Ireland's cause with the French executive. Romance is inverted here too when Biddy attempts to get Needham to marry her for "we know too much about each other" to which Needham replies, "Well, I might do worse. But not much worse" (302–3), causing its intended comic effect. However, such a happy event is not to be as both Biddy and Needham are captured by French officers and sentenced to death by firing squad. As Biddy is led to her death, she cries:

> I hope that my death will be a warning to all who in the future may depend on the generosity of the English Government ... I die the death of a traitor; no one will ever breathe a prayer for my soul's repose, nor shed a tear ... my countrymen will say "here lie the remains of the notorious informer, Curse her-curse her!" (306)

Biddy's death as informer feeds into the sense of visceral pleasure at her comeuppance, just as Needham, who has attempted to get Grace to show him mercy is also dragged out to meet his fate. Shots are fired and the two dispatched, while Grace and Donal board the French schooner bound for France in Ireland's cause.

3.5   Comic Works—*For The Land She Loved* (1915)

Bourke's later '98 play *For The Land She Loved* is also a succinct play in the melodramatic style and also establishes the comedy of the courting couple early in the first act; on this occasion, with Sheila DeLacey and Dermot McMahon. Sheila is Betsy Gray's maid, who is described as the heroine of Ballinahinch and daughter of Squire Gray, the Governor General of Down. Dermot is ambiguously named as a local patriot, and the two first met at Matt McGrath's blacksmith forge. Dermot and the others have been speaking of making and hiding pikes for the Rising, when Sheila comes upon them. Not knowing Dermot, banter ensues:

Sheila: ... now it strikes me I've seen that face before
Dermot: ... ye may have; if my memory sarves me right, I have got this face a mighty long time. (318)

Sheila immediately begins to look awry at this 'boy of the right sort,' and on Matt's telling her of his oratorical skills, "he can spake like a book," she bites back, "'Bedad an' it's the book that's mighty hard to close" (318). When Sheila leaves, Dermot offers his services, "Ye wouldn't care to be after takin' a poor boy with ye." Sheila refuses before damning him with faint praise, "it's late an' I suppose it's better to have some kind of a man; so I'll let you come" (320). The comedy of the courting couple from the lower classes is embedded quickly, and in many respects Sheila and Dermot are a more well-developed comedy couple and conventionally stronger than Ned and Kitty in *When Wexford Rose*. That being said, Sheila and Dermot's love sparring also foreshadows the duplicitous and dark turn of events following closely behind. In similar fashion again to *WWR*, the villain of this play is also a dangerous woman. Lady Nugent (who, on one playbill at least, is listed as being in the Secret Service) has her own despicable union with the local commander of the yeomanry, Colonel Johnston. He in turn is seeking Betsy's hand in marriage. Lady Nugent (whose father is the commander in chief of the King's troops in Ulster) is in love with General Robert Munro, a United Irishman. When she learns that Munro has given his heart to Betsy, not surprisingly, she vows revenge. In formulaic style Sheila and Dermot's courtin' is mirrored by Munro and Betsy's love affair, and as is conventional the lower orders carry the comic weight of those structures. Towards the end of the first act, comic violence and pain erupt when Lady Nugent, in league with Colonel Johnston succeeds in framing Munro for the murder (which she has committed) of Betsy Gray's father. Such despicable self-serving acts are again designed primarily to incite the pleasurable ire of the Queen's as popular audience.

In act two Sheila is busy plotting and planning for Munro's release from imprisonment on Lady Nugent's trumped-up charges. While Betsy's plan to free Munro is patently unworkable, Sheila persuades her mistress to her own thinking as to how best to save the master. While Sheila plots the details for the escape with Dermot, their romantic antics are not far away. Dermot tells her his mother wants him to marry the tailor's daughter Kathleen Nevin, to which Sheila spits back:

Sheila: So your mother wants a colleen to keep her lasy son ... an' let him sit in the corner spakin' wid all the people who whould chance comin an' you would tell them how they would free Ireland ... but don't aix ye to do it

Dermot: Well, says she to me, she's the purtiest girl in the parish.
           Nonsense, says I she's not a patch on Sheila DeLacey
Sheila: Here out ye go ... don't think I 'd let an omadhaun like you
           be after bossin me
Dermot: ... So here I am to ask ye to become Mrs Dermot McMahon
Sheila: Well now, you mustn't drink nor smoke, nor aix me where I'm
           going if I may want to go out to the town. Give me up all the
           money and possessions ye have, an' I must always have my
           own way. Have a nice pony and trap and have nothing to do,
           and have a servant to help me to do it. Well I think I would be
           satisfied with that
Dermot: Well look here, me girl it's not marryin' ye should be. You
           should be in heaven wid all the other women who has a mind
           like ye. (330)

This set piece between the two works the comedy of courtship very well
here. Sheila's tongue-in-cheek bargaining for her hand and Dermot's
wooing turned wry commentary creates a strong comic scene with ironic
undertones. Sheila's postponement of marriage also signals back the
trope of lack or deferment to the other plays under discussion. While the
sparked love sparring between the two continues as the act progresses,
the scene quickly switches to Colonel Johnston's attempts to persuade
Betsy to marry him. When she refuses with, "Surely you are not going to
make war on a defenceless woman?" He replies, "Yes, by heavens, I mean
to have you here and now" (332). He seizes her, aided by his soldiers who
grapple with Betsy. She screams; Dermot rushes in and wrestles with
them, throwing the soldiers off Betsy. Sheila appears suddenly, brandishing a pistol at Johnston and crying, "Stir a foot and I'll blow you and your
bloodhounds to the devil" (332). Later, Lady Nugent ridicules Colonel
Johnston for letting Betsy Grey escape, "Why Colonel, have you made
another blunder? Oh! You Officers of the King, where are your brains?"
(333). The insult must have brought some pleasure to a Queen's audience, even as it is out of the mouth of the villain herself. Sheila and
Dermot's concerted efforts to save Munro from the firing squad by taking
the bullets from the executioners' guns succeed. Shots ring out and
Munro falls to the ground, whereupon Johnston kicks him and then
attempts to embrace Betsy as Lady Nugent physically restrains her. Munro
jumps to his feet; Johnston *dashes* him with his sword and attempts to get
away with Betsy, at which point Dermot, Sheila and others end the act by

threatening the violence of pikes and pistols to the gathered soldiers. Comic violence, pain with the threat of further aggression, brings these scenes to an end. Comic patterning continues to be wrought by courtship games of the lower orders; with the servants ingeniously saving their masters and by the comic action of outmanoeuvring the enemy forces. Over and again, the woman's virtue is hooked to that of the nation as the act closes out on a 'quick picture' creating moments of high tension, comic action and pleasurable hatred for the audience.

Act three repeats the comic melodramatic formula well; Betsy Gray is being held captive for Johnston in Lady Nugent's house. Johnston and Nugent plan to lure Munro to the house and to shoot him. They spy Sheila who has overheard them. Lady Nugent cries "Set the house ablaze and pitch her into the flames" to which Sheila responds "stir one foot and I shall brain you with this iron bar" (344). Sheila is attacked; she deals Johnston a blow and is shot in the arm by Lady Nugent. Dermot 'rushes in' and 'throws off' Johnston who has grabbed Sheila again. The day is saved by Matt the blacksmith's entrance, threatening to use a pike on the enemy. Lady Nugent blames Colonel Johnston for the country's being "in a state of rebellion through the cruelty of such men as you" (348), which seems to suggest that she has some feelings for Ireland's cause; however, there is room for dark comic irony in the playing to thrill up hatred in the audience. Once more Johnston and Lady Nugent attempt to spirit Betsy away on a ship bound for America (sound familiar?), where he intends to force matrimony on her, and once more they are thwarted by Munro and the peasants wielding pikes. In the final act, there is some talk of the bravery of Sheila, fighting for and with Munro, and of Lady Nugent, who is somewhat forgiven for her actions as she "is only a woman" (350). The juxtaposition of Sheila's bravery and Lady Nugent's villainy would seem to cast Lady Nugent as weak because of her sex, while Sheila escapes that insult. That said, as the play draws to a close, Sheila and Dermot play fight for a time before finally declaring their love for one another. Dermot is jealous of Sheila's dealings with a sergeant during the rescue of Munro the previous night:

Dermot: Ye may go and stay with the Sergeant, I'll not have any man's leavin's, off ye go now
Sheila: Well I may tell ye, my boy that you are not fit to wipe the Sergeant's boots … and what are you, a jealous man, that's no good to a colleen like me. Here, give me them two bags of ammunition for the boys and I'll bid ye farewell for ever

Dermot: Don't lose your temper, my darlin, sure I'd like to be after teasin' ye to show ye how much I love you

Shelia: Now do ye mane that, Dermot, well I'll never lave ye, and we'll fight together for poor ould Ireland to-day at Ballinahinch (*They embrace*). (352)

With their romance settled and marriage implied at least, the exchange of jealousy for reconciliation in the face of battle offers a little light relief before quickly turning as Betsy calls Irishwomen to arms despite Munro's protestations that the battlefield is no place for a woman. As with Mary Doyle and Kitty Cassidy in *WWR*, Betsy is strong in battle. When asked by Johnston (who has since deserted and is in disguise) who led the rebels in battle, Dermot replies "No man sir, No Man at all." The men were led by a girl, a girl with the "courage of a lion … and her dark eyes flashed like a lance as she led us on against the hated foe" (354). In the final scene of the play, the tide has turned against the rebels and the battle against the Red Coats rages on. In the midst of this fighting, Lady Nugent is attempting to signal to the British to aid them in overthrowing the rebels. Betsy accuses her of being a spy, and they fight for the love of the man that Lady Nugent lost and for Betsy's murdered father. A duel with pistols is had first, and then with swords. Betsy kills Lady Nugent as the comeuppance that she so richly deserves in the melodramatic politic; the villain and British spy is dead. However, the play turns quickly to tragedy when a further skirmish occurs between Munro and Colonel Bruce (a British officer). Betsy steps between the two and is killed by both swords. The green flag is drawn across her body as Betsy, murdered by both sides, dies for the cause. The men kneel and make the sign of the cross.

3.6   Comic Lines

This chapter has dealt with the broad formula of romance, nation and class as a formulaic apparatus and as a series of themes running through the plays. As the analysis points up, those motifs are interwoven into the fabric of the form. At times they clearly signal to a distinct theme, at other times the motifs overlap or merge through the flow of the works. The analysis also makes clear how the comedy is working across those plotline patterns in order to draw attention to its modes of expression and its function in relationship to those motifs. As suggested at the beginning of the chapter, these explorations reveal the scope of comic expression in the plays. Working across the motifs, that scope incudes the comedy of courtship and the satirical beat operating in the works. It reveals the centrality of the comedy couple as double act and indicates what agencies there may be for the comic women moving along and across its borders. It traces the extent of comic movement from light to dark in the larger scope of the political melodramas, and it draws out class structures as comic material. It describes comic violence and intention including the hooking of nation to virtue in the works and it focuses on the dark playful power of the female villain-informer. The potential for what that scope may reveal involves other comic conversations and brings in the discussions for the next chapter, which takes as its focus some central means of comic playing to deepen the analyses here. To that end the next chapter considers the comedy double act in some depth so as to understand the function of the device through the selected plays. Female comic agency both in and out of the double act is also interrogated to thread deeper meaning for comic women along its porous edges. The discussion then moves on to what purpose there may be when examining comic intention in relationship to the experience of a popular audience. The chapter takes time to consider comic women in detail toward a consideration of those women on Irish popular stages, moving towards the heart of the book. Considering the role and function of comic women during the period illuminates into some very dark corners what comic women might say and do within the permissions and constraints of the Irish popular political stage. The concluding discussions draw out the loose association of ideas considered to formulate the comic everywoman and what that signifies in and for theatre practice.

NOTE

1. One of P.J. Bourke's earliest plays was an adaptation of *Kathleen Mavourneen*, which played in the Father Mathew Hall and made it to the boards of the Queen's in 1910. As a protoplay, it operates as a series of scenes, and as romance principally, although it plays along, and with class lines in so doing. There are some strong comedic scenes in the work; as when Kathleen discusses daily life with her superior Dorothy Kavanagh, and the gravedigger scene is an exercise in Irish commedia; however as the play, while relational, is not thematically built on the politics of the patriotic melodramas in the same way, it falls outside the remit here.

Bibliography

Bourke, P.J. 1991a. When Wexford Rose. In *For the Land They Loved: Irish Political Melodramas 1890–1925*, ed. Cheryl Herr. Syracuse: Syracuse University Press.

———. 1991b. For the Land She Loved. In *For the Land They Loved: Irish Political Melodramas 1890–1925*, ed. Cheryl Herr. Syracuse: Syracuse University Press.

Whitbread, J.W. 1991a. Lord Edward or '98. In *For the Land They Loved: Irish Political Melodramas 1890–1925*, ed. Cheryl Herr. Syracuse: Syracuse University Press.

———. 1991b. Wolfe Tone. In *For the Land They Loved: Irish Political Melodramas 1890–1925*, ed. Cheryl Herr. Syracuse: Syracuse University Press.

Fig. 4.1 The Comic Everywoman, courtesy of Sean Mullery

Fig. 4.2 Marian, courtesy of Sean Mullery

CHAPTER 4

Comic Women (Some Men Are Also Involved)

Abstract This chapter links the comic analyses of the plays, drawn out in the last chapter, and allies those considerations of expression and purpose to some central ideas in humorous thought. The discussion begins with the comic mode of incongruity and its relationship to the comic device of the double act. It applies that thinking to the comedy couple in the plays, and to the women playing along its borders, before connecting the device to its comic intentions for the audience. The conversation then moves on towards an in-depth consideration of comic women in popular theatre and in Irish political melodrama. Finally, it proposes the comic everywoman as a means of encapsulating Irish comic women in the popular houses and in dialectical relationship with her audience.

Keywords Double act • Benign comedy • Tragi-comic • Satire • Slapstick • Reversals • Comic Everywoman

© The Author(s) 2018
S. Colleary, *The Comic Everywoman in Irish Popular Theatre*,
Palgrave Studies in Comedy,
https://Doi.org/10.1007/978-3-030-02008-8_4

4.1   You Can't Live With Him … the Comic Duo in Irish Political Melodrama

The last chapter spent some time drawing out the comic structures, mechanics and possibilities at work through the selected plays and the interwoven motifs of romance, nation and class. This chapter allies those considerations to a series of discussions, which link the analyses to comic thinking on their expression and purpose. The chapter takes this route in order to deepen the comic discussion and to direct the conversation towards an in-depth consideration of women in popular theatre and in Irish political melodrama. Towards the end of the chapter, the loose formulation of the comic everywoman is proposed as a means of encapsulating the comic woman in the popular houses. It is also sketched as a way through which to explore how the Irish comic woman could speak to her counterpart in the everyday world. The discussion begins with a central pillar in comic thinking: that of incongruity, before moving on to discuss the double act, its nature and function and the comic ideas that flow through the device. This flow will then branch out to a discussion of female comic agency in the plays, charting comic women in popular theatre towards the ideas inherent in the comic everywoman.

Peter Berger takes some time to discuss comic experience in philosophy, tracing the debates back to Francis Hutcheson, through Kant and Hegel, and to Bergson and Swabey to illuminate incongruity in comic worlds.[1] The thinking is well rehearsed as one of the principal theories of comic thought, and its explication in the literature is ample. Using Pascal and Kant, John Morreall's formula is useful: "we live in an orderly world where we have come to expect certain patterns among things … when we experience something that doesn't fit these patterns, that violates our expectations, we laugh."[2] Similarly David Farley-Hills describes the comic as that which "arises from the incongruities between opposed ways of regarding the same ideas or images."[3] Or as Simon Critchley pithily suggests, incongruous humour describes the "experience of a felt incongruity between what we know or expect to be the case, and what actually takes place in the joke, gag, jest or blague: 'Did you see me at Princess Diana's funeral? I was the one who started the Mexican wave.'"[4] Allied to the idea of incongruity is that of suddenness; Farley-Hills describes it as the element of "surprise [which] in conjunction with incongruity provide[s] us with the essential elements of the comic."[5] He notes that the idea is also well established in comic theory, suggesting that its importance becomes "obvious when we appreciate the need for the incongruous images or ideas to be present before the mind at virtually the same instant."[6] For Farley-Hills, suddenness brings to the mind equally valid yet oppositional thoughts or interpretations instantaneously, creating the required tension for laughter. Critchley describes the idea of suddenness in a relational if different way. Drawing on Kant (again), Critchley describes joke telling as comic patterning of "duration and instant." As listeners we commit to being told a funny story or joke, we know that the punchline (through repetition and or digression) is on its way, whether up close or in the distance, which is in itself an anticipatory pleasure. When it comes, the duration of the telling snaps into the instant, and we laugh.[7] Comic theory and mechanics then, combine to produce audience laughter.

The jostling together of contradictory ideas or feelings (to paraphrase William Hazlitt), allied with the workings of comic timing, can be useful when examining how the servant couples operate in the patriotic melodramas. As a kind of comic double act, they function as device for carrying much of the comedy to the audience. Broadly, what we understand as the double act, is still familiar to performance, grown out of variety entertainment in its modern guise and often defined in physical, intellectual or class difference. The comedian Ken Dodd once described the physical disparities between Laurel and Hardy as the 'perfect symmetry of comic incongruity.'[8] While physical contrasts can be a defining feature, there are others, including "status and quick-wittedness;"[9] as Oliver Double notes, the classic variety act was rooted in the "contrasting status of the two performers … laughter echoe[d] from the clash of one against the other."[10] M. Harrison describes the act in a related way, where "one usually present[s] the funny lines while the other acts as his straight man, feed or stooge."[11] This is again similar to Double's point that inherent to the double act is the idea of the straight man, who "played higher status" [often class related] and "the funny man was… the working-class underling."[12] Finally, Louise Peacock describes particular types of comic duos including the "sparring double act … in constant competition [or as] partners, often working to a common goal."[13] She cites Morecambe and Wise's fluid movement between sparring and supportive as "verbal comedy and gentle slapstick."[14] For Peacock, the comedy is found in the "differences in attitudes and outlooks of the two halves."[15] Those differences may lie in status, or intelligence or in class or wealth, that which is clearly recognisable, but not so divisive as to impede both, when needed, working to a shared objective.[16] Interestingly, Peacock makes the point that double acts with a gendered dynamic are rarely seen, the idea of male dominance over a woman, especially in physical terms destroys laughter. However, gender does play a role in the servants' relationships, and implicitly in the upper orders, although not in Peacock's terms. That said, whether in opposition or in concert, the double act is embedded in incongruous thought, creating ambivalence and comic tension, which can only be resolved through laughter. However, as Farley-Hills notes, that resolution is temporary; while the audience may eventually choose one side over another, by comic design, the audience are required to 'suspend judgement' until that time arrives.[17] As comic device then, the pair represents incongruity to the audience, that is, the push and shove of difference, be it social, physical or other, as integral to their construction. In this way they are the embodiment of comic incongruity; they signify the clash of contradictory ideas that lies at the heart of incongruous humour. The suspension of judgement allows the comedic patterns to repeat multiple times depending on the comic intent as the double act play out oppositional or co-conspiratorial roles for the audience.

Understanding incongruity and its relationship to the double act helps to recognise the comic relationship between the servants in the political melodramas. Within the comedy of courtship, misunderstanding creates hurt feelings and ruffled pride, spilling over into faux aggressive comedy, an ersatz anger as the lovers take verbal pot shots at each another. The servants court or fight one another, sometimes with soft banter and sometimes with satirical barb and jealous bite, all the while engaged, until married (and sometimes after), in romantic combat. In this way and under the romance motif, the servants are an antagonistic duo set up through the comic structure of courtship and misunderstanding, as with Kitty and Thady in *Lord Edward* and Peggy and Shane in *Wolfe Tone*. Their misunderstandings can be resolved or deferred quickly, or protracted for comedic effect depending on the comic balance between antagonism and the need to work together in the plays. Misunderstanding may not even be necessary to start the fight, think of Sheila and Dermot early in *For The Land She Loved* (*FTLSL*), where Dermot's cockiness is enough to ruffle Sheila's feathers. The verbal sparring can also be quite soft as part of the wooing act; imagine early in *When Wexford Rose (WWR)* where Kitty resists Ned's advances playfully, as, together, they prepare for war. At times other forces overrun romance. Ned and Kitty's (and, to a lesser extent, Sheila and Dermot's), play fights are quickly invaded by the reality of war and is exemplary, as discussed in chapter two, of the emotional switching inherent to the form. Nation temporarily overrides romance, which sets up a layered functional structure within which the double act can work. The atmospherics of danger follow Ned and Kitty's (as example) playful teasing very quickly. In that sense their double act courtship dynamics also work as light relief against the immediacy of the darker drama unfolding. Thady and Kitty do similar in *Lord Edward* when working together to protect the master, or in gentle opposition as they fight; these moments often offset the imminent tragic tone in the play. That sense of switching between lighter and darker moments, where the tragic is close on the heels of the comic, is not as structurally evident with Peggy and Shane in *Wolfe Tone*. The pair work in accord for large measures of the play, so that comic action and dramatic moments are embedded in the work. However, the play's tonality as a whole tends to be less tragic and more hopeful (not so for the informer), so that I suggest the comic relief is not as overt as in other plays. Sheila and Dermot's play fights and barbs as oppositional, can also signal the tragic at close quarters; towards the end of the play in particular they work that switch for the audience, where jealousy gives way to love, to patriotism and to the play's final sacrificial scenes.

The trope of physical or slapstick humour, comic violence and comic pain are patterned through the plays also. While not all the physicality and action scenes are built to be comic to the exclusion of darker and more realistic tones, the comic potential is present in the text for a good portion of the action scenes. Under all three motifs of romance, nation and class, aggressive comedy happens. In *Lord Edward* Thady and Kitty's oppositional beginnings incorporate his fond remembrance of Kitty's physical abuses towards him as a child, which sets the tone for the comic violence to come. The pair can act with and without each other in some scenes or as witness in others. Large action pieces include Kitty's getting into perilous waters at the hands of the Crown. Her fight to escape manhandling is aided by Thady's arrival, where together they make several attempts to do comic violence and inflict comic pain to best the enemy. In *Wolf Tone*, Peggy and Shane are also actively involved in comic violence or the threat of it. Shane sets up the comic pain to come when he enacts knockabout violence on Rafferty early in the play. In the double, the pair threaten or enact comic violence and mete out comic pain, while large action scenes where nation or virtue (or both) is threatened, see the pair brandish, struggle and fight off foes. *WWR* offers a different structure than the preceding works, and as a result, the threat and enactment of comic violence and pain feels more realistic stylistically and tonally, so the comic structures, while present, are somewhat muted. *FTLSL* represents something of a return to comic convention. Sheila and Dermot more faithfully represent the comic duo; they also fight the foe, for each other and their betters. When in antagonistic mode the pair can set up the idea of comic violence amongst themselves. In accord, literally and figuratively at times (as when they are acting out of the double), the pair threaten or enact comic violence and inflicts comic pain on their enemies. They can do so for themselves and for their betters. As with the other duos, getting the better of the Crown, even temporarily, while saving their masters comedically enacts the triumph of good over ill in the moral universe of the play, while also speaking to the servants' 'knowing' better than those above their station. Winning the day also presents the pair's trials and victories in a class-conscious light for a Queen's audience.

While the motif of class operates through comic violence, it also works in other ways. Class is apparent in the plays' hierarchies, and the comedy can work to subvert those structures, as the action scenes make plain. However the act of saving their masters also occurs outside that action. On a number of occasions and acting together or apart, Thady and Kitty save Lord Edward and Pamela from their enemies. Hiding Lord Edward in a fireplace or inside a mattress, running the gauntlet with the Crown to get dispatches one to another; the pair risk their own skins for their betters in many ways. So too Peggy and Shane in *Wolfe Tone* rescue both their masters from the nefarious deeds of others to stop their wedding, or from financial and social embarrassment. They both spend time rescuing their mistress from the threat of sexual violence and protecting Wolfe Tone from harm. As already noted, the women in *WWR* are strong; while Kitty and Ned's working together is threaded through the play, Kitty and Mary also work in tandem to save their masters, significantly in the offstage battlefield. In *FTLSL*, both together and separately, Dermot and Sheila are busy plotting escape for their imprisoned master and saving Betsy from the threat of sexual violence patterned on a number of occasions through the play. Plotting and planning for their superiors' benefit and risking their necks in the process demonstrates again how the comedy double act, even when they are apart but in accord, have quicker wits than the 'quality,' they are resourceful, clever and loyal; these qualities all flow through the device of the comic duo. Their comedy signals to the subversion of class hierarchies, as they are the major architects of triumph over evil under the melodramatic sign for the audience.

Finally and structurally, often (but not always) near the 'saving the masters' trope, there is a satirical impulse at work across the motifs. A principal mode is that of comic defiance, usually at the forces of the Crown and the villain-informer, and this is at work across all the plays under discussion. Whether it belongs to Thady's ridicule of Major Sirr, Kitty and Mary's defiance of Needham or Ned's playing cat and mouse with Biddy, the thread runs right through the succession of plays. There are a multitude of exchanges working in the satirical mode and channelled through the double act as comic device. There are a multitude of exchanges that work outside the double act. Romance as attack is familiar as the expected outcome or resolution is always, however, deferred in the offing. The attitude of attack when clearly levelled at the enemy, usually the British forces or their agents, works to actively ridicule, deride and demean the target, creating a comedy of insults for the oppressors in the plays. Satirical barrages again set up the victory however temporary over the unjust forces at work in the political melodramas, connecting through comedy with the collective wish fulfilment of a popular nationalist audience.

4.2   You Can Live Without Him—Comic Women Outside the Double

The discussion so far has centred on the comic device of the double act, although I have traced how the women, across the plays can move in and out of that structure at times. I want to expand on that discussion here to explore how the women work comic agency, and to what degree, outside the doubling and interwoven across the plays' central motifs of romance, nation and class. The earlier works allow for the characters' temporary escape as with Kitty in *Lord Edward*; the instance of her disguise as a soldier is initially successful and comic, but the men reproach her actions and she quickly reverts to her stock permissions. So too, Kitty's defiance is plain in mocking the agents of the Crown; at times in sexual peril, she can threaten or actualise comic violence on her foes, which signal her ingenuity, her knowingness, her defiance and her triumph. Acting alone creates moments of comic agency, often, but not always as satellite to her rescue by the male counterpart. Even her defeat at playing a soldier gives her a moment of comic power, which threatens the male sphere, before she is recuperated. In *Wolfe Tone*, Peggy's character type is more outspoken than Kitty's, and from early in the play, she speaks (both in and out of the doubling) to the upper echelons with a confidence and ease that disregards hierarchical class structures. She is also not afraid of a melee; she attacks the villain-informers as she attempts to save her masters; in so doing she is threatened (as is her mistress) with physical and sexual harm. While acting on her own Peggy can be satirical, and she uses comic violence or its threat, in service of her betters. As with Kitty, although Peggy is stronger in some respects, she has access to comic agency, where she subverts social caste, fights for victory over the Crown and knows better than her superiors. As with Kitty the escape is temporary, and she is constrained from saving the day; the victory for nation and with it, 'virtue' ultimately belongs to the men.

In *WWR*, Kitty acts out of the double frequently, and she along with Mary Doyle to a lesser extent harness the satirical or mocking voice when in conflict with the Crown. On the whole the women are depicted as strong, even heroic, in battle. Even the stilted heroine Grace Bassett grows levels of agency as the play progresses. The telling of Mary and Kitty's bravery in war does not happen onstage, but in the diegetic space, which signals under the heroic rather than comic sign for the audience. The play does not have as large a series of action scenes as its predecessors, and structurally the storytelling is something of a departure from the convention of onstage comic action. In addition the women along with the men save their masters, and the way that it told to an audience tones down its comic power. However, other scenes, which deal with the same subject matter, are alive to their comic purpose. There is still strong sense of the women as the lower orders being smarter than their superiors, and of victory for nation through comic violence. Mary also works the intertwining of virtue and nation when saving her mistress, while in another scene the men alone save virtue, so again something of a break with traditional structure as discussed in these pages is occurring. Another departure sees Mary and Kitty start to resemble a double act outside the traditional pairing. Mary begins to diverge into the hero *type* with Kitty as the trusted, somewhat comic sidekick, mirroring in relief the male hero and trusted servant in the plays. Interestingly, the comic sidekick lives on, while Mary as hero(ine) is dispatched. In this doubling, their mockery of foe is defiant, and insulting, while their willingness to do physical harm is evident. However at times the violence in this play carries more realistic overtones, perhaps because of the storytelling structure employed and perhaps also because the play overall moves towards a more realistic telling of events although, as noted comic violence still pertains. As a result, it's possible to argue that the work is operating less under the structurally conventional comedic sign. That said, this double act as fitting loosely within, while subverting stock types and belonging to the women only has access to the centre of comic power on the stage. Likewise, in *FTLSL* Sheila also acts out of the double when attempting to save her master and mistress, by creating a workable plan and helping to save Munro from the firing squad. Saving Betsy from the threat of sexual violence as the imperilled woman in the fight for nation through the working of more conventional action scenes also gives Sheila comic agency momentarily although again, the weight of saving the day belongs to the men. While others discuss Sheila's bravery, ambiguously emphasising her superiority over the villain and in some ways reflecting Kitty and Mary's stories in the diegetic space, her action scenes are staged for the most part. She enacts her comic agency by visiting comic violence and pain or its threat on the enemy on a number of occasions through the play. Although not as satirical (except perhaps with Dermot) as others before her, Sheila defies, insults and fights her way through the plot; her ingenuity outshines her mistress as she outwits or challenges the enemy, through the comic structure of the plays.

While Grace Bassett in *WWR* emphasises something akin to character development, in a sense representing another realistic shift in the formal structure of type, the female villain is another variation on a theme. The role was more usually gifted to the male actor, however Whitbread employed the character of Lady Rose Sydney as the villain in *Sarsfield* as far back as 1904. So too, Bourke has utilised Biddy Nolan and Lady Nugent as villainous women in the later plays of *WWR* and *FTLSL*. Biddy Nolan, the notorious informer, brings rebels to the noose for money. In a despicable union with Needham (she even tries to get him to marry her), they attempt to defeat the rebels to achieve their own pecuniary and amorous ends. Lady Nugent works in much the same vein, as the scorned woman who will stop at nothing to seek revenge on Betsy and Munro. Much like Biddy and in another despicable union with Johnson as agent of the Crown, she carries out murderous acts with impunity. Biddy's informer status is more marked than Lady Nugent's who, for the majority of the play operates at a subtler remove. In many respects both despicable unions operate as inverse to the comic duo of the servants, to Kitty and Mary and to the hero-servant stock relationship in that they are working to very different ends. Neither Biddy nor Lady Nugent are constrained by the double act however, and move in and out of that structure easily, which gives them access to the power of comic agency as villains within the plays' structures. At times both satirise those they are in league with, which may have brought a Queen's audience into transitory alignment with their own comic disdain for the enemy. Working on their own, as they carry out their deeds, some of which involve sexual threat, both Biddy and Lady Nugent are mocking to those about them, extracting pleasurable hatred by design from the audience. Perhaps Biddy's plots and counterplots along with ruthless disregard for her people and country were especially deserving of the ire of the Gods, however, Lady Nugent was also just such a character that a Queen's audience loved to hate. Like Biddy, who is shot for her misdeeds, Lady Nugent too meets her just desserts, this time at the hands of Betsy herself who runs her through with a sword. The joy of hating the villain-informer as a function of comic intent brands the plays with the nationalist stamp in very clear terms. Social caste seem buried here too under the overarching sign of melodrama, that of triumph over evil, but not before severally raising the pleasurable bile in the audience craw.

4.3   Comic Patterns

While the discussion to now has connected comic expression to comic device and what that suggests about the purpose of the comedy for an audience, this section connects other comic thought to those purposes. It examines ideas of comic function as it relates to the analyses in order to deepen the discussion of comic intent in relationship to the audience. The section then bends that consideration toward an in-depth discussion of comic women in popular theatre. To begin the conversation then, Peter Berger suggests that benign comedy is intended to "evoke pleasure ... provid[ing] no real threat to the social order ... close to ordinary life ... though it takes out of it whatever is painful or threatening."[18] The thinking is useful to describe the servants' romantic relationships although it does not fully account for them. On the other hand, Berger's notion of satirical comedy where "aggressive intent becomes the central motif of comic expression"[19] suggests that satire necessitates a target of attack and can be tonally malicious regardless of any high-minded moral or principle. Such oppositional descriptions of benign and satirical comedy would readily imply that there can be no such thing as benevolent satire. However, Berger does suggest that satire can operate on a spectrum of severities, with the proviso that "satire that is overly gentle, liquidates itself."[20] Berger rightly identifies the paradox of benign satire as unachievable as comic expression; however, the servants (and, to a much lesser degree, the gentry) manage to balance the benign and the satirical in a number of ways. As discussed, the exchanges between the servants in all the plays can become quite aggressive and satirical to various degrees and with various degrees of irony attached. Even when they are in concert towards a common goal, they can move in and out of an antagonistic attitude with one another. To my mind, that balancing act describes benign satire as long as the comic equilibrium between the two poles is sustained and harmonised. There is also something to be said here about satire as comic intent; Berger suggests that satire as attack "are part of an *agenda* on the part of the satirist" and are very dependent on "a particular audience, in a particular social context."[21] Broadly, an audience familiar with the genre of the patriotic plays and melodramatic form would understand the 'benevolent satire' of the servants as familiar precursor to its ultimate resolution. In that sense the comedy is created through the incongruous structure of the duo, and its effect is designed to entertain the audience as enjoyable, escapist, even innocuous comedy. The satirist's (be it writer *or* performer in the melodramas) agenda may well be to evoke audience laughter from the couples' 'cut and thrust' whilst knowing that comic resolution is in the offing through an 'understanding' reached or equally the institution of marriage. The deferrals keep the comic tension working through the servants' relationships. The comedy is wrought by actively *not* resolving those conflicts, and that irresolution provides, for multiple ways to play out the comic potential for both sides, although the women's deferral of marriage is a point to which I will return a little later on. By comparison, Berger's description of the tragi-comic mode as "comedy that consoles," where the tragic "is not banished, not defied, not absorbed [but] momentarily suspended,"[22] is also at work through the servants' relationships. Another way to describe its hybrid nature is, as Karl Guthke argues, through audience response; those who "laugh with one eye and weep with the other."[23] The idea of comic relief works through some of the servants' scenes where the comedy of the courtin' couple is turned by the emotional switch; that switch is necessitated by the dramatic turn in tone or mood within the play structures. In this way, the lighter moments offset the dark that must follow in a tragi-comic world. In a sense, the tragi-comic is often the comi-tragic in the plays. That is, the laughter as relief comes in advance of the imminent tragic tones to follow. However, within the switching structure of the form, it's less useful to create any sort of concrete linearity. Guthke's description of "twinning the contraries" in the moment probably best describes the way that comic relief works through, rather than before or after (although that does occur) the tragic tones. That said and working through the servants' relationships, the tragi-comic structure acts as a "comic breathing space," a fleeting release of tension between the tears for the audience.

Allied with benign satire and the tragi-comic mode, slapstick comedy is also at work, understood here as "physical humour of a robust and a hyperbolised nature, where stunts, acrobatics, pain and violence are standard features."[24] Peacock argues that defining slapstick has been a limited exercise in academia, and she traces its derivation to *Commedia dell'arte* and before. She suggests a general understanding as including some if not all of the following:

> A central double act; comic pain and comic violence; falling and tripping; malicious props … throwing of objects … and stunts and acrobatics. Many of these are conveyed through the physical skill and mastery of the performer and are supported by sound effects.[25]

Peacock again centralises the incongruous nature of the double act to slapstick as comic device, which can work appositionally or in accord when attacked by outside forces to create comic worlds of violence and pain. In similar vein, for Eric Weitz the audience enjoys the "safely delivered brutality" of comic violence where "we trust that no one really gets hurt and that even the victims are in on the joke."[26] Slapstick gags, according to Donald Crafton, can disrupt the cause and effect of narrative to act as "atemporal bursts of violence and or hedonism that are …. gratifying" for the audience.[27] An audiences' enjoyment of comic violence is central; however, Peacock addresses *intentional* performed violence and pain on stage more specifically. She suggests that where intent is concerned, and this is not always the case, the question of morality necessarily becomes involved. Peacock makes the point that "broadly put, if the pain appears deserved we are more likely to laugh than if it appears to be unjust."[28] Moral justice then, where audience perception recognises that the victim richly deserves comic punishment and pain, affects laughter as response. As to purpose, Peacock argues that "status plays a key role in whether or not we find slapstick funny … as an audience, we find it funny to see the mighty fallen or to see dignity upset."[29] As has been seen through the plays, comic violence and pain are enacted through the action scenes that the servants (both in and out of the double) and others including the heroes (sometimes the heroines) become embroiled in. They inflict comic brutality on their enemies and in turn have violence perpetrated against them. The audience find enjoyment in vicariously living through the triumphs of the just and the deserved suffering of the corrupt. Here again is the victory of good over evil as central to the ethical world of political melodrama. That triumph is brought about temporarily through comic action scenes, where the servants are victorious in the aid of their betters, and where they *know* better than their 'betters' in defeat of the enemy. Further, Peacock's discussion of moral justice where the audience laugh at punishment 'richly deserved,' where the mighty have fallen, also speaks in very clear terms to how the violence and pain are operating the politics of nation for comic effect in the plays. In parallel, the politics of class work in a different way through comic violence, for implicitly or explicitly the servants upset hegemony on both sides of the divide for laughter. Finally, to my mind, Crafton's point about slapstick's capacity to disrupt the cause and effect of narrative is countered by the subtextual freedoms offered in playing out the comic potential in these scenes. There is plenty of room to co-create alternative or competing narratives with an audience through comic action, and this is something to which I will return in the next chapter.

Berger's satire, unhooked from the function of benevolence, is also in action through the works. Extending the earlier double act discussion, Berger borrows from Northop Frye's work on satire as 'militant irony'; an "attitude of attack that is part of a campaign against someone or something," with ironic undertones invested in "saying one thing and meaning another."[30] The use of satire is, as discussed earlier, conditioned by the *satirists'* agenda, and its purposes for attack are various and many in the larger comic structures of the plays. Throughout, the satirical edge is harnessed to mock the enemy as assault, which can actualise into the committal of comic violence and pain. Yet the enemy is not without the same weaponry, also at work to various degrees and purposes of attack and significantly, the mockery of Biddy and Lady Nugent as villain-informers is heavily weighted under the satirical sign. Working with their willing cohorts as despicable unions, Biddy and Lady Nugent employ Berger's satirical mode to insult and ridicule their opposition. Both also threaten (at times the threat is sexual) and commit comic violence and pain, yet their acts work on an audience in an unexpected way. Although they dole out cruelty with impunity, their actions incite that pleasurable hatred discussed, so that there is laughter, fuelled by the knowledge that in formulaic style, they will reap what they sow. Both also work outside the double, where satire is their continued weapon of choice. For Elaine Aston and Ian Clarke in their work on villainess's in Victorian melodrama, their nefarious self-serving actions produce strong reaction [here] in the patriotic plays, as the "character an audience loved to hate."[31] As such, the villain-informers constitute a powerful if malevolent force on the stage as darkly comic women. That comic agency has access to the central structures of these plays, through text and subtext, through language and its performance undercurrents in relationship with the audience. Their satirical powers may win over an audience, as when the women mock colonial forces; however, in the end, the moral world of the play owns the mode. Its ethical universe belongs to those who are being oppressed. When the villain-informers are winning and when they are losing, they incite the hatred of a popular nationalist audience. How they navigate that relationship is something that I will draw out a little later, for there is almost nothing better than the pleasurable identification felt in punishing the villain-informer for her wickedness; it's almost, as Aston and Clarke argue, as pleasurable as watching her commit those crimes.[32]

4.4   The Comic Unreality Principle

Before I move on to the final consideration of comic women on popular stages and the comic everywoman in this chapter, I want to expand on the earlier discussion of comic violence for a few moments as it informs that discussion. Both Crafton and Weitz discuss the idea of slapstick as that which is pleasurable to an audience, where the violence seems unreal, which frees an audience to laughter. Broadly, their thinking aligns with Peacock's view that slapstick as comic expression allows an audience a space to feel rebellious at a safe distance from any real consequence. In Peacock's view the idea of safe space necessitates a comic frame when discussing performed violence on stage. A comic frame is integral in order to signal to an audience that empathy is not required as response to the violence witnessed; rather, laughter is the appropriate reaction. In order to open an audience to the perception of violence in this way, a comic frame must be built in as that "lack of reality," that Weitz and Crafton also refer to, for too much reality collapses the frame. So, the lack of reality sets up a sense of detachment from the violence, creating a safe comic distance as key to produce laughter.[33] The idea of the 'unreal space' where comic violence flouts, defeats and inverts hegemony on stage to produce laughter resonates with a carnivalesque vision. Drawing here from Mikhail Bakhtin, carnival can be understood as a socially sanctioned space of play where the normal rule of daily life becomes temporarily inverted, turned upside down, where the mechanised structures of a culture are dispensed with if only for a brief time and hegemony and power is (seen to be) denied through mockery and laughter.[34] This inverted space is one which turns the social world on its head, producing a carnivalesque vision "mocking the rule and order of the everyday"[35] denying its constraints, its hegemony and its power. In this unreal place, victory temporarily belongs to those without access to power in the material world. For those involved the carnival frame creates a safe space through which to play out wish fulfilment in the imaginary realm, one that is protected from any real consequence. In this way, the carnival or inverted space utilises the lack of reality, and comic distance to produce laughter, in other words the carnival space invokes a comic frame. The idea connects to Peacock's comic frame necessary for slapstick, in the sense that comic violence operates within a similar comic frame. More broadly, that comic frame, is operating beyond the device of slapstick solely and across the landscape of the political plays. This broader working of the comic frame is also in relationship to the inverted space of carnival where the oppressor, is always denied or temporarily overthrown. Working through inversions, lensed with the comic frame, the servants use comic violence to defeat the enemy; more broadly, time and again, their knowingness and their ingenuity save their social caste superiors, outwitting the coloniser by multiple means and orchestrating the villains' ultimate downfall. So, when called upon, the inverted space of carnival hooks in with the comic frame, signalling as the non-serious mode, as ambivalent, as distancing technique for laughter. An audience decoding the performance understands the unreality principle, where 'hedged round' (as Johan Huizinga would have it), it is safe to laugh at authority, to find pleasure in its being usurped, to enjoy the overthrow of its constraints. To my mind the inverted space and the comic frame work to those permissive ends, a safe space for those who without access to power play out wish fulfilment through the prism of the patriotic plays. Further, the political melodramas are stamped very clearly with the nationalist emblem, working in the inverted space, and in the non-serious mode for comedy. Yet, that comic ambivalence can also communicate the *reality* principle with an audience. In other words, comic ambivalence, allows both unreality and versions or agendas of reality to co-exist. It is up to an audience to decode that ambivalence which can politicise and subvert the comedy to its own ends even as it signals the non-serious mode to the audience. Comic ambivalence must also work through the conditions of production and reception where, as Boucicault learned much earlier, a popular audience involves a cross-class and affiliative cohort. Reversals of the real world, the unreality of that space, its non-serious mode, can accommodate the gradations of nationalist sentiment across those cohorts, where its very unreality may have added for some, to its attractions. In the end, the performance frame, which inverts the space and employs comedy to support those inversions, is working across the political melodramas and underpins the discussion of comic women to follow.

4.5   Twisting the Comic Sense—The Comic Everywoman

The discussion so far has examined the range of comic structures at work across the plays as formulaic patterns, lensed through the overall performance frame, when signalling the non-serious mode, and so far connected in some detail to all three motifs. I want to discuss romance in some further detail here as it connects in significant ways to women and comedy in melodramatic worlds. Conventionally, the institution of marriage was staple for women on Victorian stages. Tracing comic worlds back through new and old, Dmitri Nikulin argues that comic drama "stresses shared action oriented towards a good ending—or, we might say, a happy ending—and a resolution of a given conflict."[36] From a philosophical perspective, Nikulin argues that comic resolution is like dialectical reasoning in that 'allosensus' is reached; that is where the opposing sides come to know each other without either being 'sublated,' and where conflicts are resolved through a reconciliatory ending.[37] Ending happily in comedy brought with it the institution of marriage, and the audience welcome the desired outcome, or to borrow from Northop Frye, the 'this should be' moment.[38] In similar vein, Susan Carlson writes that structures in comic drama tend to move from the presentation of the status quo, an inversion that upsets or threatens that order, and reversion to the reestablishment of that order in some way. Distinctly, Peter Brooks discusses melodramatic endings as "very seldom [being] the drive towered erotic union, so typically the case in comedy, which if sometimes present is no more than another indicator of virtue's right to reward."[39] For Brooks, melodramatic endings are centrally involved with virtue's conquest over evil. There is not:

> as in comedy the emergence of a new society formed around the untied young couple ridded of the impediment represented by the blocking figure from the older generation but rather a reforming of the old society of innocence, which has now driven out the threat to its existence and reaffirmed its values.[40]

Unlike Nikulin's more egalitarian idea of reconciliation, and in parallel with Brooks, Carlson finds that women in comedy have functioned in narrow permissive straights, as a "basic inversion and a generally happy ending … women are allowed their brilliance, freedom and power in comedy only because the genre has built in safe guards."[41] In disruption, women can take on dominance for "women in power are funny because they are so out of the ordinary." However, such power does not hold, an audience may enjoy its novelty and may deliberate on the notion of female power, but it is a transitory reversal, made safe by the performance frame of inversion and by the comic distance made. As the 'close in' looms, women are assimilated back into the form's conventional modes and reconciliatory ends. Carlson uses Edit Kern to make the point that power for women is built in fantasy, a dream where those locked out of influence have temporary access to power in the space and can triumph over their oppressors. However, that denial or displacement of hegemony through laughter belongs only to an imagined world. So Carlson believes that as non-mimetic representation, women within that imaginary space are ultimately part of a system whose overall intent is bent on maintaining the existing state of affairs.[42] Brooks makes an analogous point. Drawing from Booth and Eric Bentley, Brook believes that melodrama belongs to a dream world also, providing the possibilities of "saying, what is in 'real life' unsayable." Its world may seem to work with clear hierarchies, yet for that, Brooks argues that it is an egalitarian space, as its aesthetic ethic calls for "victory over repression." Its performative means to achieve that end is overt, so that "*nothing* is understood and *everything* is overstated … [where] characters tend to say, directly and explicitly their moral judgments on the world."[43] In that space, the unsayable becomes sayable, where the virtuous or innocent can confront her powerful oppressor with moral certainties, notwithstanding class or gender lines, utterances which could not be said on an "earlier stage, nor still on a nobler stage, nor within the codes of society."[44] That said, comic disruption and saying the unsayable both revert to the restoration of values, within the ethical universe where good triumphs over evil, or in the restatement of the status quo. Either way both assimilate and constrain the women as ending.

The relationship of women to power and comic agency in the imaginary or dream space across both forms speaks naturally to the carnival space and the comic frame. I have already discussed the inverted space to explore how the patriotic plays are working through that performance frame, when signalling the non-serious mode. However, while Carlson and Brooks (under his own terms) acknowledge that traditional comic endings can be acts of reversion and for Carlson specifically "work against women," she also connects the significance of the inverted space to comic women in the theatre. She discusses the anthropologist Victor Turner's work on cultural ritual and theatre. For Turner:

> Liminal phenomena may on occasion, portray the inversion or reversal of secular, mundane reality and social structure. But liminoid phenomena are not merely reversive, they are often subversive, representing radical critiques of the central structure and proposing alternative models.[45]

In his view, the theatre space and *act* of performance can deepen the potency of the inversion, forging "new paradigms and models which invert or subvert the old."[46] That said, while Turner believes that acts of theatrical inversion can challenge or make change to the existing structure, this happens only in particularised socio-political circumstances. In recognition, Carlson proposes that Turner's conceptualisations, which present the possibility for "both the reality and the *rarity* of change," can, from within the inverted space, critique or challenge the social order by means of comic performance. In other words, the inverted space can represent powerful subversive site[s] for women on stage; the ambivalence of inversion, and the comic frame, which signals the non-serious mode, holds the potential for comic women to challenge convention, both formally and socially; yet those same structures also de facto pressurise women into recuperation. Still yet for Carlson the rebellious power that women can briefly hold in comedy's reversals has the albeit limited potential in Turner's terms to "serve as models for real women."[47]

Any challenge to existing structures from within must find a performative means of doing so, which brings the conversation back to the comic women in the political melodramas. Joseph Holloway wrote of Boucicault's *Arrah-na-Pogue* at the Queen's in 1898, that the audience knew every line of the text and the Irish actors' byplay in their roles, so that the players were left in no doubt if they gave less than that which the play warranted.[48] While only a glimpse, the review gives an indication both of text and of its playing between the lines in relationship with the audience. In a sense this connects to Tracey Davis' definition of a body of plays and performances wherein meaning is communicated to the audience through "iteration, revision, citation and incorporation" of well-known scripts, performance and formal patterns.[49] That theatrical and performative fluidity is also underpinned by intertheatrical knowledge, which Jacky Bratton describes as a "web of mutual understanding between … audiences and their players [as]… knowingness about playing that spans a lifetime or more." For Bratton:

> entertainments … that are performed within a single theatrical tradition are more or less interdependent … they are uttered in a language, shared by successive generations, which includes not only speech and the systems of the stage … but also genres, conventions and very importantly memory.[50]

Broadly, it is within this bank of theatrical and intertheatrical knowledge, that which is new or different in the intertheatrical field, of innovation and creative invention, is filtered and understood.[51] On many levels, the patriotic plays work within this thinking. They were popular because of their very familiarity to an audience, their 'knowingness' about the repertoire and its ways of playing over time. Yet, these ideas also extend the thinking beyond that of the script alone, depended upon as artefact when researching distant texts and where performance is difficult to reproduce or access. Instead, the text becomes that of performance text as Richard Schechner describes it encompassing "all that happens during a performance, both onstage and off including audience participation [for]… a performance is much different and more complex than the staging of a playtext."[52] Davis, Bratton and Schechner are all, in their ways, speaking to the core idea of the performance text. Katherine Newey's discussion on the theatrical device of metatheatricality as used by Victorian actresses adds specifics to the melodramatic aspect. She argues that "metatheatrical awareness" is one of melodrama's main means of communication with its audience. Contrary to thinking about metatheatre as literary or avant-garde, Newey argues that metatheatrical devices were popular and familiar to a melodramatic audience, constituting a:

> self-referential sign system, which exploits the playfulness and artfulness of the theatre … the spectator understands and accepts these codes and conventions, not simply as theatrical ploys, but as an approach to theatrical representation which is deliberately self-conscious and self-reflexive.[53]

Self-reflexive performance as that which refers back to itself, which can point to the artificiality of the theatre and theatrical representation, opens the written text to multiple ways of playing and interpretation by an audience. As example, in Aston and Clarke's view, such means are available to Victorian villainesses, those "dangerous women...[working] with their male accomplices .... who took the lead and constituted a fierce opponent."[54] In their reading she is "powerful, calculating and remorseless,"[55] who, as actress, employed her comic *cognito* to produce laughter which "might not be apparent in the script, but [which] are caused by the different intonation of twisting the sense."[56] Understanding performance text in this way as the totality of expressive means in acts of communication with an audience brings us back in a way to what Sos Eltis describes as the 'unpredictability' and 'immediacy' of the performance space in Victorian theatre, having the potential to "destabilise or complicate established notions ...[or]moral orthodoxies."[57] In my terms understanding the Victorian stage space as unpredictable, with the potential to challenge existing social structures, speaks back to my earlier discussion of agency in the liminoid space and in the *act* of performance for comic women. The subversive possibility of the carnivalesque inversion, which is operating through comic ambivalence, is signalled through the performance text; that is the totality of expressive means that a comic woman has in her possession, within the bounds of the performance frame in relationship to her audience. Self-referentially playing with theatrical representation, twisting the comic sense to make other meanings also speaks to Bratton and Davis' discussion for innovation within banks of theatrical and intertheatrical knowledge with a co-creative audience. The matrix of understanding between an audience and its players encapsulates its knowingness of the repertoire and all that it entails. The matrix also recognises the totality of the performance text as expressive means. The comic woman is embedded in these structures, utilising their fullness as comic cognito in relationship with her audience. For me then, herein lies the possibility for reading Irish comic women on Irish popular stages.

This loose association of ideas begins to shape the idea of the comic everywoman on the patriotic stage, working within a bank of theatrical knowledge and a matrix of understanding between the audience and its comic players. The set of performance ideas here bring to life the comic woman on those stages, in a way that the playtext alone cannot. The formula acts as key to unlock the texts under discussion from a distance: understanding those performance permissions, restraints and possibilities offer new ways for reading comic women in Irish popular theatre. On some levels too the formula is influenced by the everyman trope itself; ubiquitous in literature, drama and film. Linked to the medieval morality play, the everyman is loosely characterised by its typicality, its everydayness and its familiarity to the viewer. It represents that which is common or ordinary, placed in extraordinary circumstances and attempting to survive. Usually within the male preserve, the spirit of the everyman shadows the patriotic plays, built to speak to the world of the everyday. The ethical universe of melodrama is also built to speak of battle between good and ill for the everyman, and the comic woman within its cast of characters is working in the same way; she is stock, typical, identifiable and familiar to the audience. She is known from within those banks of intertheatrical and cultural knowledge circulating and percolating. She is borrowed from temporal progressions of cultural representation as Irish female identity. She is Sydney Owenson's "wild Irish girl," or staged peasant beauty, witty and brave, nationalistic, sentimental and loyal.[58] That popular cultural presence requires control; she is often depicted as "close to nature" under the imperial gaze and in need of its steadying hand to contain her wild, or innocent or sexually charged ways. Yet, such representations differed radically depending on audience, so she could be read as emblematic of assured British superiority in London, or as passionate nationalism in Ireland.[59] As with other stages and genres, and discussed earlier, female signification in popular theatre could not escape the hooking of women to nation. Staged female identity could not outrun the role of Mother Ireland, so that women on popular stages often represented and were interpreted as the sexualised and politicised body over which the struggle for Irish freedom played out.[60] For me the comic everywoman is built from those familiarised symbols of Irish female identity, working within the bank of theatrical knowledge and innovation, within the performance tradition and text as totality of expressive means, and finally embedded in the matrix of understanding between her and her audience. Made from all this substance, built from the stuff of the everywoman, embedded in all her characteristic and performative ideas the comic everywoman represents female identity when playing out and signifying under the comic sign. Ultimately, the condition of the comic everywoman defines the relationship with her audience.

In these pages and between the melodramatic and comic recuperations, the comic everywoman plays for her audience. In the political melodramas the nationalist message may be written large in the script, but the scripts themselves are open to multiple ways of playing and interpretation for an audience. In this inverted space, through the comic frame, and along the double act borders, the comic everywoman acts out her comedy world; there is less of the more traditional melodramatic woman as victim about her, although she does not fully escape being rescued one way or another by the men. That does not mean to say that she could not play with that 'rescue' for comic effect in relationship to her audience. She can deliberately orchestrate misunderstanding in love; she can obfuscate the marriage proposal and defer the inevitability of an 'understanding' while pointing up her worth for the proposed transaction. She has room to play ambiguously with infidelity and can eschew courtship for the business of war. She can upset status and collapse class boundaries with her comic tongue. She can emblazon with nationalist sentiment, and in its cause, she can outwit and outmanoeuvre the British crown. Her knowingness perceives her masters' limitations and her ingenuity aids and saves them. Her comic violence can triumph over the enemy when virtue and country are under threat; those actions also quietly provide room to co-create other narratives with an audience. She can mock, she can deride and she can defy the enemy (and with less edge her love interest) by multiple means, and she can cross gender boundaries to threaten the male space. Such access to comic power and its means of playing is mirrored, on the other side by villainy, which challenges the moral world of the plays. That darker comic power also fits the formula of the comic everywoman in relief, playing out female representation under the villainous sign. Working mostly in the satirical mode, she can be all manner of violent at times, and attacking nationalist sentiment incites pleasurable hatred by design in the audience. However the villain-informer can also play self-referentially, within her relationship to the Crown. Her self-servedness as comic ambivalence allows her the space to mock the enemy as well as the hero. While she is branded with the overt signage of evil, she also has the ability to play between those lines to point up the nature of the colonial relationship to its slave. She also flirts with marriage to the Crown that opens up a myriad of ways to play with the master-slave relationship for the audience. And the villain-informer as comic everywoman can play with the colonised and sexualised body of Irish female identity in the same way as the other staged representations can with an audience. The comic everywoman can give the pleasure of benign humour with a satirical wink. She can make comic poignancy in advance of the darker clouds on the horizon, and she can attack and deride that which is unjust in the play world. Access to that comic power is played through the totality of expression, through the performance text and frame, with comic ambivalence signalling the non-serious mode. To my mind, that comic agency has the power to speak to its audiences and to

speak of the world beyond the theatre walls. Through the popular performance means discussed here, the comic everywoman can signify the power
of nationalist sentiment writ large in the works. From within those trans-
missions she can also speak to the condition of marriage for women, to the
constraints of social class for women and to the myriad of social and cultural perceptions and coda that seek to label women as *less* or *other* through
their class and their gender. I argue that that performative comic signalling
is present on the popular stages and that the very popularity of those stages
ensured the message travelled. While the argument is, to say again, necessarily mediated by the contingencies of the theatrical and cultural space for
women, that is not to say that the comic everywoman did not harness the
power of the stage to make multiple meaning with her audience. And those
audiences were plentiful in the city and along the theatrical axis by the late
nineteenth century in Ireland.[61]

The native dramas whether new, or revived, were mass entertainment
with access to market; be it Cork, Belfast or through the rolling nomadic
fit-up circuit, thousands of people spent Dublin evenings "howling for
the informer's blood at The Queens."[62] While a Queen's audience has
been well documented, gender demographics are sketched; however, the
tradition of mixed sex patronage attending respectable variety houses in
Dublin has been broadly recognised. So too the broad understanding of
both working and middle-class audiences attending the Queen's and
other patented theatres in the city implies the same.[63] In late Victorian
melodrama, Aston and Clarke position strong, often comic, female characters on the popular stage at a time when the "unfixing of femininity"
was occurring in more fashionable theatres and arenas of cultural thought.
Discussions were centring on the post-Ibsenite New Woman figure in
relationship to societal debate about suffrage, independence and sexual
liberation. The staging of strong women with comic power, in their view
adds to the "key debate of the period in a popular culture context."[64] In
a related way, Meaney et al. discuss the first decades of the twentieth
century, noting the rise of "conservative backlash against the forces of
social change which had been gaining force since the 1890s" in Ireland.
Meaney argues that despite the reactionary forces at play, spaces of "cultural and sexual dissonance and of occasion political resistance" did exist
for both working- and middle-class women during the period.[65] As
already discussed and important to reiterate, this does not lessen the
understanding here that the women were constrained by the form and by
the cultural coda. Aston, Clarke and Eltis all mediate their discussion

with the objectification of staged women whether by audience or management who were being "sensationalised for prurient and masculinist ends."[66] In an Irish context these ideas are complicated by the representation of women where "sexual identity and national identity are mutually dependent,"[67] so its arguable that the body of the Irish comic woman in popular drama is sexualised and politicised by the producer and read for one, for the other or for both by the male and female consumer in the popular plays. That said, Meaney takes issues with those who assume that working- and middle-class women as consumers were "simply dupes," passive in the exchange between the cultural product, whether in her reckoning, cinema or in mine that of popular theatre, and that points of dissent were available even for those without access to "highly esteemed cultural forms such as the theatre and literary fiction."[68]

While Meaney's discussion is speaking of access to perceptions of 'high' art, working and middle-class women attended the popular houses in the first decades of the new century. I suggest that the comic everywoman had the means and the motive to speak to her audiences through the legibility of signs that incorporate the totality of the performance experience. In this way the comic everywoman can access the transitory power of the stage to construct alternative 'sense' within the bounds of the melodramatic form and the performance frame. Imagining those moments is one thing; thinking about their practice is another, which brings me to the final strand of analysis that informs this study. The next chapter then takes a practice-as-research approach towards comic women in the patriotic plays as popular theatre. It discusses my involvement with popular theatre practice as a series of workshops, scripting and performances, and is useful to the final discussion of comic women in *practice* through selected playworks. While the practice-as-research lens is discussed from many practitioner and academic standpoints, for my uses, Robin Nelson's argument is useful. He advocates for learning through practice, necessarily entailing "knowledge, which is a matter of doing rather than abstractly conceived … a kind of practical knowing-in-doing, which is at the heart of PaR."[69] Testing the works in practice could articulate that *knowing-in-doing* which Nelson speaks of. From a practice standpoint I wanted to see if I could uncover that which Eltis talks about when she discusses her academic study, as wishing to "make legible once more some of the dramatic gestures, interconnections, references and meaning available in various forms to their contemporary audiences."[70] Finally Robin Nelson uses the term *clew* here meaning "the thread of the researcher's doing-thinking" as she moves through the comparable but differing processes of practice and research. They are not one and the same as Nelson points out; art works are "complex, and multi-layered," while the research enquiry requires its own clarity; however, practice does evidence the research inquiry. The idea of the *clew* fits well into the parameters of the next chapter, which speaks to work I carried out as practice, and as practice-as-research towards a number of final performances in 2016. However, for me the *clew* works as a conceptual thread also, one that places the comic everywoman centre stage and in relation to her everyday 'self' outside the walls of the theatre. Teasing out those *clews* between the comic everywoman and her 'like' in the world offers a performative glimpse into that hidden relationship 'twisting the sense' to that which is already received.

NOTES

1. Peter Berger, *Redeeming Laughter: The Comic Dimension of Human Experience* (Berlin: Walter De Gruyter, 1997), pp. 24–35.
2. John Morreall, 'A New Theory of Laughter,' in *The Philosophy of Laughter and Humour*, ed. by John Morreall (New York: State University of New York, 1987), p. 130.
3. David Farley-Hills, *The Comic in Renaissance Comedy* (Basingstoke: Macmillan Press, 1981), p. 20.
4. Simon Critchley, *On Humour*, Thinking in Action (Oxon: Routledge, 2002), pp. 3–6.
5. Farley-Hills, *The Comic in Renaissance Comedy*, p. 21.
6. Farley-Hills, *The Comic in Renaissance Comedy*, pp. 21–2.
7. Simon Critchley, *On Humour*, pp. 6–7.
8. Ken Dodd quoted in Louise Peacock, *Slapstick and Comic Performance: Comedy and Pain* (Basingstoke: Palgrave, 2014), p. 50.
9. Louise Peacock, *Slapstick and Comic Performance*, p. 53.
10. Oliver Double, *Britain had Talent* (Oxon: Palgrave, 2012), pp. 116–7.
11. Louise Peacock, *Slapstick and Comic Performance*, p. 50.
12. Oliver Double, *Britain had Talent*, pp. 116–7.
13. Louise Peacock, *Slapstick and Comic Performance*, pp. 53–4.
14. Louise Peacock, *Slapstick and Comic Performance*, p. 54.
15. Louise Peacock, *Slapstick and Comic Performance*, p. 58.
16. Louise Peacock, *Slapstick and Comic Performance*, p. 56.
17. David Farley-Hills, *The Comic in Renaissance Comedy*, p. 24.
18. Peter Berger, *Redeeming Laughter*, p. 101.
19. Peter Berger, *Redeeming Laughter*, p. 157.
20. Peter Berger, *Redeeming Laughter*, p. 158.

21. Peter Berger, *Redeeming Laughter*, p. 158.
22. Peter Berger, *Redeeming Laughter*, p. 118.
23. Karl Guthke quoted in Gail Finney, 'Little Miss Sunshine and the Avoidance of Tragedy,' in *Gender and Humour: Interdisciplinary and International Perspectives*, ed. by Delia Chiaro and Raffaella Baccolini (Abingdon: Routledge, 2014), p. 228.
24. Andrew Stott, *Comedy* (Oxon: Routledge, 2005), p. 92.
25. Louise Peacock, *Slapstick and Comic Performance*, pp. 31–32.
26. Eric Weitz, *Theatre and Laughter* (London: Palgrave, 2016), p. 43.
27. David Crafton cited in Andrew Stott, *Comedy*, p. 95.
28. Louise Peacock, *Slapstick and Comic Performance*, p. 11.
29. Louise Peacock, *Slapstick and Comic Performance*, pp. 38–9.
30. Peter Berger, *Redeeming Laughter*, p. 157.
31. Elaine Aston and Ian Clarke, 'The Dangerous Women of Melvillean Melodrama,' in *New Theatre Quarterly*, (12:45), (1996), p. 35.
32. Elaine Aston and Ian Clarke, 'The Dangerous Women of Melvillean Melodrama,' p. 35.
33. Louise Peacock, *Slapstick and Comic Performance*, pp. 25–6.
34. Russian theorist Mikhail Bakhtin introduced the theory of carnival in his book *Rabelais and His World*, written in the 1930s and published in 1965. Embodied in the free space of marketplace, although sanctioned by the hegemonic order, the laughter of carnival can be represented as ambivalence towards official culture, so we understand that 'in the carnival, dogma, hegemony and authority are dispersed through ridicule and laughter.' Within the itinerary of carnival festivities, we encounter a ludic celebration of macabre humour (pregnant Death) and the grotesque body, which Bakhtin believed, contrary to Gnostic ideology, held the promise of true salvation. Bakhtin's belief in 'grotesque realism' proclaims to the world that the power of carnivalistic laughter is trans-temporal and universal but that the carnival free space of play is the place in which the 'drama of the body' is enacted by and for the populace. Bakhtin argued for the "The drama of birth, coitus, death, growing, eating drinking, and evacuation. This corporeal drama applies not to the private, individual body, but rather to the larger collective one of the folk." It is within the free space and free time, that is, the carnival space of play that a 'myth of ambivalence' is created that denies death in and through the power of laughter. For further discussions on Bakhtin's concept of carnival, see Mikhail Bakhtin, *Rabelais and his World*, trans. by Helene Iswolsky, (Bloomington: Indiana University Press, 1984). Also, see Renate Lachmann, Raoul Eshelman and Marc Davis, 'Bakhtin and Carnival: Culture as Counter-Culture,' *Cultural Critique*, 11 (1988–1989), pp. 124–30.

35. Susanne Colleary, *Performance and Identity in Irish Stand Up Comedy: The Comic 'i'* (Hampshire: Palgrave, 2015), p. 84.

36. Dmitri Nikulin, *Comedy, Seriously: A Philosophical Study*, (New York: Palgrave, 2014), p. x.

37. Nikulin, *Comedy, Seriously*, p. 54.

38. Northrop Frye quoted in Nikulin, *Comedy, Seriously*, p. 166n.

39. Peter Brooks, *The Melodramatic Imagination: Balzac, Henry James, Melodrama, and the Mode of Excess* (Yale: Yale University Press, 1995), p. 32.

40. Peter Brooks, *The Melodramatic Imagination*, p. 32.

41. Susan Carlson, *Women in Comedy: Rewriting the British Theatrical Tradition* (Ann Arbor: University of Michigan Press, 1991), pp. 17; 20.

42. Susan Carlson, *Women in Comedy*, pp. 18–20.

43. Peter Brooks, *The Melodramatic Imagination*, pp. 36, 41.

44. Peter Brooks, *The Melodramatic Imagination*, pp. 41–2.

45. Victor Turner quoted in Michael Bristol, *Carnival and Theatre: Plebeian Culture and the Structure of Authority in Renaissance England* (New York: Routledge, 1989), p. 38.

46. Victor Turner quoted in Susan Carlson, *Women in Comedy*, p. 20.

47. Susan Carlson, *Women in Comedy*, p. 19.

48. Joseph Holloway quoted in Paige Reynolds, *Modernism, Drama, and the Audience for Irish Spectacle*, (Cambridge: Cambridge University Press, 2007), p. 23.

49. Tracey Davis quoted in Sos Eltis, *Acts of Desire: Women and Sex on Stage 1800–1930* (Oxford: Oxford University Press, 2013), p. 2.

50. Jacky Bratton quoted in Sos Eltis, *Acts of Desire*, p. 2.

51. Tracey Davis quoted in Sos Eltis, *Acts of Desire*, p. 2.

52. Richard Schechner, *Between Theater and Anthropology* (Philadelphia: University of Pennsylvania Press, 1985), p. 22.

53. Katherine Newey, 'Melodrama and Metatheatre: Theatricality in the 19th Century Theatre,' in *Journal of Dramatic Theory and Criticism*, Spring 1997, p. 85.

54. Elaine Aston and Ian Clarke, 'The Dangerous Women of Melvillean Melodrama,' p. 31

55. Elaine Aston and Ian Clarke, 'The Dangerous Women of Melvillean Melodrama,' p. 33.

56. Frederick Melville cited in Elaine Aston and Ian Clarke, 'The Dangerous Women of Melvillean Melodrama,' p. 34.

57. Sos Eltis, *Acts of Desire*, p. 7.

58. See Geraldine Meaney et al., *Reading the Irish Woman: Studies in Cultural Encounter and Exchange, 1714–1960* (Liverpool: Liverpool University Press, 2013), p. 186.

59. For a more comprehensive discussion on Irish representation through the colonial lens, see Mary Trotter, *Ireland's National Theaters: Political Performance and the Origins of the Irish Dramatic Movement* (Syracuse N.Y.: Syracuse University Press, 2001), pp. 43–63.
60. Mary Trotter, *Ireland's National Theaters*, pp. 62–70.
61. R.F. Foster notes the "lively theatrical culture of nationalist theatre in Cork and Belfast" at the turn of the century, see Foster, *Vivid Faces: The Revolutionary Generation in the 1890–1923* (UK: Penguin Random House, 2015), p. 79.
62. Christopher Morash, *A History of Irish Theatre1601–2000* (Cambridge: Cambridge University Press, 2002), p. 129.
63. Meaney et al. discuss popular cultural production and consumption by working- and middle-class women during the period. She cites Rosamund Jacobs' diaries which chronicle her theatre going activities in the 1930s often combining plays at the Gate, the Olympia and the Abbey Theatre, suggesting that middle-class women consumers crossed "high culture and popular entertainment," for an evening's pursuit. See Geraldine Meaney et al., *Reading the Irish Woman*, p. 204. For a comprehensive discussion of Irish audiences during the period, see Joan Fitzpatrick Dean, *Riot and Great Anger: Stage Censorship in 20th Century Ireland* (Wisconsin: University of Wisconsin, 2004), and Paige Reynolds, *Modernism, Drama, and the Audience for Irish Spectacle.*
64. Allardyce Nicoll cited in Elaine Aston and Ian Clarke, 'The Dangerous Women of Melvillean Melodrama,' p. 32.
65. Geraldine Meaney et al., *Reading the Irish Woman*, p. 180.
66. Elaine Aston and Ian Clarke, 'The Dangerous Women of Melvillean Melodrama,' p. 32.
67. Geraldine Meaney, *Sex and Nation; Women in Irish Culture and Politics* (Dublin: Attic Press, 1991), p. 3.
68. Geraldine Meaney et al., *Reading the Irish Woman*, p. 181.
69. Robin Nelson, *Practice as Research in the Arts: Principles, Protocols, Pedagogies, Resistances*, Ed. Robin Nelson (Hampshire: Palgrave, 2013), pp. 8–9.
70. Sos Eltis, *Acts of Desire*, p. 1.

BIBLIOGRAPHY

Aston, Elaine, and Ian Clarke. 1996. The Dangerous Woman of Melvillean Melodrama. *New Theatre Quarterly* 12 (45): 30–42.
Bakhtin, Mikhail. 1984. *Rabelais and His World*, Trans. Helene Iswolsky. Bloomington: Indiana University Press.
Berger, Peter. 1997. *Redeeming Laughter: The Comic Dimension of Human Experience*. Berlin: Walter De Gruyter.

Bristol, Michael. 1989. *Carnival and Theatre: Plebeian Culture and the Structure of Authority in Renaissance England*. New York: Routledge.

Brooks, Peter. 1995. *The Melodramatic Imagination: Balzac, Henry James, Melodrama, and the Mode of Excess*. Yale: Yale University Press.

Carlson, Susan. 1991. *Women in Comedy: Rewriting the British Theatrical Tradition*. Ann Arbor: University of Michigan Press.

Colleary, Susanne. 2015. *Performance and Identity in Irish Stand-Up Comedy: The Comic 'i'*. Hampshire: Palgrave.

Critchley, Simon. 2002. *On Humour, Thinking in Action*. Oxon: Routledge.

Dean, Joan Fitzpatrick. 2004. *Riot and Great Anger: Stage Censorship in Twentieth Century Ireland*. Wisconsin: University of Wisconsin.

Double, Oliver. 2012. *Britain Had Talent*. Oxon: Palgrave.

Eltis, Sos. 2013. *Acts of Desire: Women and Sex on Stage 1800–1930*. Oxford: Oxford University Press.

Farley-Hills, David. 1981. *The Comic in Renaissance Comedy*. Basingstoke: Macmillan Press.

Finney, Gail. 2014. Little Miss Sunshine and the Avoidance of Tragedy. In *Gender and Humour: Interdisciplinary and International Perspectives*, ed. Delia Chiaro and Raffaella Baccolini. Abingdon: Routledge.

Foster, R.F. 2015. *Vivid Faces: The Revolutionary Generation in the 1890–1923*. UK: Penguin Random House.

Lachmann, Renate, Raoul Eshelman, and Marc Davis. 1988–1989. Bakhtin and Carnival: Culture as Counter—Culture. *Cultural Critique* 11: 124–130.

Meaney, Geraldine. 1991. *Sex and Nation; Women in Irish Culture and Politics*. Dublin: Attic Press.

Meaney, Geraldine, Mary O'Dowd, and Bernadette Whelan. 2013. *Reading the Irish Woman: Studies in Cultural Encounter and Exchange, 1714–1960*. Liverpool: Liverpool University Press.

Morash, Christopher. 2002. *A History of Irish Theatre, 1601–2000*. Cambridge: Cambridge University Press.

Morreall, John. 1987. A New Theory of Laughter. In *The Philosophy of Laughter and Humour*, ed. John Morreall. New York: State University of New York.

Nelson, Robin. 2013. *Practice as Research in the Arts: Principles, Protocols, Pedagogies, Resistances*, ed. Robin Nelson. Hampshire: Palgrave.

Nikulin, Dmitri. 2014. *Comedy, Seriously: A Philosophical Study*. New York: Palgrave.

Newey, Katherine. 1997. Melodrama and Metatheatre: Theatricality in the 19th Century Theatre. *Journal of Dramatic Theory and Criticism* 12 (1): 87.

Peacock, Louise. 2014. *Slapstick and Comic Performance: Comedy and Pain*. Basingstoke: Palgrave.

Reynolds, Paige. 2007. *Modernism, Drama, and the Audience for Irish Spectacle*. Cambridge: Cambridge University Press.

Schechner, Richard. 1985. *Between Theater and Anthropology.* Philadelphia: University of Pennsylvania Press.

Stott, Andrew. 2005. *Comedy.* Oxon: Routledge.

Trotter, Mary. 2001. *Ireland's National Theaters: Political Performance and the Origins of the Irish Dramatic Movement.* Syracuse: Syracuse University Press.

Weitz, Eric. 2016. *Theatre and Laughter.* London: Palgrave.

CHAPTER 5

The Comic Everywoman

Abstract This chapter identifies a practice-as-research approach to comic women on Irish popular stages. It initially outlines the terms of the research practice and discusses the exploratory workshop and rehearsal processes, tracing that journey through to the final performances. The empirical work connects to the melodramatic aesthetics discussed in the second chapter and works in parallel to the comic analyses and discussions in the third and fourth chapters. The outcomes are discussed as illuminating popular performance, comic performance and comic women in popular performance. The final conversation focuses on the comic everywoman, as she encapsulates the performative *clew* between staged comic identities for women on Irish popular stages and her everyday self.

Keywords Practice-as-research • Workshops • Ways of playing • Feminist • Comedy • Comic Everywoman

5.1 Background

When I was researching performance histories and popular culture for my book on Irish stand-up comedy, I found Irish music hall and tripped over Irish political melodrama. These performance histories are underwritten in Irish discourses, and I knew that I wanted to stage music hall and the patriotic plays to understand how they worked, and what they meant,

S. Colleary, *The Comic Everywoman in Irish Popular Theatre*,
Palgrave Studies in Comedy,
https://doi.org/10.1007/978-3-030-02008-8_5

then and now. After a year in the making, and working with the visual artist Sue Morris, in 2016 we staged a multi-media installation entitled *Here We Are At The Risk Of Our Lives*. The work centred on the life and work of *Kitty Kelly*, a fictitious music hall star and male impersonator, or masher:

> As a central focus for an exploration of themes around the 1916 Rising—war, identity, nationality, Diaspora and emigration, gender and class, loss and mourning.[1]

While *Kitty* was forming, the seeds of the second project were sown. Initially, I discussed the 'native dramas' and their contexts with two fellow actors. After reading some scripts, we were keen to explore how the out-dated texts and stock characterisations of Irish identity would play out in the rehearsal room. With that broad church in mind, we gathered a group of actors together and created a schedule of laboratory-type workshops, which at first sketched out the summer of 2014, but eventually grew into a performance piece a full two years later. Starting from scratch, the idea was to put scene work from a selection of the plays 'on their feet,' to try and understand how they worked and to know their broad potential *as* performance. Early on in the process, we began to recognise recurrent motifs through the plays, and as the workshops became more focussed, we discovered how the native dramas worked as melodrama—its plotlines, its characters, its comic and tragic tones, its atmospherics and acting styles and its specific themes operating through the patriotic plays. We began developing an acting style or aesthetic in order to discover how to play stock character, only hinted at in the economy of the scripts. This knowledge drove us towards a melodramatic aesthetic for playing the texts. That aesthetic freed us from a superficial reading of the works and allowed us to dig deeper into what playing the scripts might actually mean as performance. The plan was to create a devised piece of theatre, built from that which we discovered and what was useful to us in the workshop and rehearsal space. That piece of theatre would draw from the patriotic plays as performance bricolage and as the means through which to interrogate popular theatre and its contexts in 1916 Dublin. We intended to perform the work as part of the 2016 centenary commemorations of the Easter Rising.

There follows here a timeline of those workshops and how they moved towards the creation of *Marian and Joseph: A Revolutionary Love Story*. By virtue of the fact that this work stretched across two years, it's important here to qualify the terms of the investigation. The nature of the project's broad objectives at the outset focussed on ways of playing melodrama and was not specifically designed with comic women in mind. However, the laboratory process soon identified the richness of the popular plays, which included but was not exclusive to the plays discussed in these pages. That thinking quite quickly brought the group to a number of performance possibilities for the devised piece, which organically it seems now, dovetailed with my research interests in popular performance, comic performance and comic women in popular performance. Research and practice began to occur simultaneously as I worked from one session to the next, and while this was happening, I began to think of wanting to write this book. So in a sense, the eye to production came first and the focus was exploratory for some time in order to capture the direction of the devised work. We continued our explorations and the discoveries made spoke to us across the melodramatic construct, its life as an aesthetic, its principal means of communication and importantly, its contradictory freedoms for women. So, in summary the focus of this chapter is not primarily on the final performances although that does inform the work, but that which was learned through the practice-as-research lens. As such the workshop and rehearsal processes speak to the duality of those evolving objectives which arrived at the performance piece. Those processes also materially inform the research outcomes gathered from the process itself. At times those sets of objectives necessarily differed, yet they also crossed one another in very real ways as Robin Nelson rightly identifies. The outcomes discussed are as a result of that exploratory process, then threaded through the rehearsal stages and onto the final performances. That process also underpins the discussion of the comic everywoman as the performative *clew* between staged comic identities for women on popular stages and her everyday self.

5.2   WORKSHOPS

Workshop One—June 2014

The first workshop was scheduled for June 2014. The plays selected were P.J. Bourke's *For The Land She Loved* (*FTLSL*) and *Kathleen Mavourneen* along with J.W. Whitbread's *Sarsfield* and *Wolfe Tone*. Having studied the plays thematically, the recurring motifs of romance, nation and class formed the basis for the first and ongoing workshops. The actors explored these themes through working with script, improvisation and attempts to physicalise the stock characters, most especially, heroes, heroines, villains and the servant class. We played scenes that spoke to all three motifs. Bourke's *Kathleen Mavourneen* played well for ideas of women and class with episodes of satirical humour; in addition one actor commented that the gravedigger scenes especially with its macabre and physical humour played like an Irish version of *Commedia D'el Arte*. The actors enjoyed *Sarsfield*, playing with the comedy of courtship and intrigue across class; the selected scene work was rich with plotting, trickery and disguise in the name of love. Ideas of folly and of class punctuated the play, although the actors underplayed elements of the scene work, understandably so, as they were trying to find their way in to an unknown acting style. I noted as much in my journal, "It needs close direction to bring out all the subtleties but they are there under the surface of the text to add nuance to the stock situation and characters …[the text also] reveals other points of class and folly."[2] Playing out speeches of nation and defeat in *Sarsfield* in a minor key punctuated the romantic melodrama, giving a nationalist focus to the play. Playing sentiment as response to stock situations necessitated (as discussed previously) emotional switching, that is, the actor having to switch quickly from one emotional state to another in order to react to his or her circumstances in the plotline. This 'switching from comic to dramatic' was visible in all the scripts we were working with and early on became a subject for discussion. The actors spoke of the difficulties at times in switching between emotional states as a way of playing. My journal recognised as much with *For The Land She Loved*. I noted that playing the heroine Betsy "requires that the actor move quickly between the display of emotional states, from love of man to love of country and back again."[3] We also spent some time playing out the threat of sexual violence or forced marriage; there was a tendency to play into comedy only, as the actors struggled with the intensity of the acting demands and the necessity for emotional switching within the form. Playing with the servants Peggy and Shane in *Wolfe Tone* provided much joy for the actors who again worked with emotional states, switching between the comedy of romance and scenes where national concerns were paramount. It was observed by all that the servants had come to Wolfe Tone's aid at several points through the play. I wrote that this way of playing demonstrated "solid comic scenes of a type—the servants who are both courting and plotting and planning on their master's … behalf [with]… hints of … violence (gun) built into the scene."[4] My notes also point out that across the plays that day, in proposing plots to save their masters, the servants were far smarter than their superiors. In addition the scenes around marriage between Peggy and Shane were feisty, loving and ambiguous, so the sense was that Peggy was more ambivalent than her mistress on the idea of entering into the institution. We also played with the use of asides in relationship to an audience and with sound effects and nationalist songs as score to the scene work. My journal also draws attention to the physical skirmishes that the actors played out in the room, noting the soap opera, cliff-hanger or silent cinema effect of the action scenes and the tableaux, in order to "carry the story and evoke strong feeling when necessary."[5] After that first session, it was clear from my own observations as well as the actors' voices that what seemed to be outdated and clichéd scripts "worked so well when they [were] up on its feet."[6] The first workshop established how well the plays worked as performance, although finding a way to play across anxieties about the hackneyed language style, negative stereotyping and an unknown form was something that was going to need work. What we did gather in a clearer way was how melodramatic acting styles necessitated the actors to quickly switch between emotional states to carry the themes of romance, nation and class. We also were beginning to understand that the switching incorporated fluidity of movement between light and dark, comic and dramatic tones in the works and that physicality (although played out badly!) was integral to the style. Embedded in those ideas of playing was the understanding of how important the action scenes were to the comedy and the drama and how they and the tableaux communicated the scene work and messaging to an audience. Finally we were also beginning to get a sense for the importance of songs and sound effects to the storytelling.

Workshop Two—July 2014

The second workshop was planned while reviewing the first workshop through video (I recorded the first session and subsequent sample workshops and rehearsals) and through my notes and concentrated on the work of Hubert O'Grady's *The Famine, The Eviction* and *Emigration*. The session was designed to work broadly under the thematic of representation and reception with the motifs of nation and class forming the spine of the workshop. I wanted to work with O'Grady's action scenes and his use of tableaux in the plays. I wished to investigate how the plays' use of stage pictures and physicality worked as performance and whether they carried any kind of social commentary.[7] I was interested in evoking a melodramatic atmosphere and considering how those atmospherics underlined the social critique inherent in O'Grady's works.[8] This was something that I was principally interested in—some kind of totality of expression represented by the physical and atmospheric landscapes, how they might work with O'Grady's plots and the turn to social commentary in the plays. While I had *The Famine* and what was available of *Emigration* (two acts are missing from the Lord Chamberlain collection), for *The Eviction*, I only had some lines of text and some stage directions to work with.[9] The idea was to use the source material as a treatment and devise how the particular scene might play. Ideas of audience reception were left until the afternoon.

We began by working with emotional states and switching between them as a warm-up for the session. For *The Famine*, the actors workshopped the Prologue, which consists of three short scenes, and concentrated on some catastrophic moments of the Irish Famine in the mid- nineteenth century. We then moved on to *The Eviction*, set roughly in the same time period and which deals with the forced removal of Irish people from their lands and homes by the British or their agents. A scene that particularly stood out that morning was the bed scene in *The Eviction* where the McMahon family are expelled from their home. Old Mrs McMahon swears a vile curse at the bailiff Rooney, she dies in her bed, which is lifted like a coffin and carried outside. While she lies in the cold, her house is taken apart, brick after brick by Rooney and his men. The second scene that worked very well was the Bog of Allen scene in *Emigration*. The play centres on the Burk family who are being forced into emigration and are on their way to Dublin to make passage on coffin ships bound for America. This is an absurdly comic and slapstick skirmish between the villains of the piece (turf pelting and falling in bog holes), who attack the Burk family, as they cross the bog. The departure for America at the end of the act was also workshopped, with Hughey (Kitty Burk's love interest) singing farewell to Ireland as the curtain slowly descends; its visual and emotive power felt poignant. The *Famine* scenes, though short and self-contained (they did not integrate into the rest of the play), were not unlike other works of Irish drama that deal with tragedy. The actors felt that these scenes were familiar to play, which may speak both to the melodramatic qualities in Irish drama and O'Grady's realistic powers in this melodrama. That said, the play's monologue by the villain Sadler (the second of the Prologue) brought with it a discussion of direct address and of the villain's use of mockery and satire as ways of baiting a nationalistic audience. The Bog of Allen scene was greatly enjoyed by the actors, for its rich veins of dark comedy and its physicality in action and as stage picture as the

Burk family finally get the upper hand. The character of Kitty is significant in the playing. She is as physical as the men and exacts plenty of comic violence on her foes, throwing them off and pelting them with turf. She has agency to act and is in no way passive in the brawl. In performing the stage directions, it was clear to the actors that they had many ways in which to play out the scene in relationship to the audience. As to whether the visuals carried social commentary, the actors were undecided, and I felt that as they had enjoyed playing the scene so much, to work to intellectualise it would be counterproductive. We left the idea open for another day. Not so for *The Eviction*. The discussion turned frequently to the idea of imagery and atmosphere in the play. The actors felt the power of the old woman being carried from her house into the snow keenly, the winter scene adding to the poignancy of the visual imagery. In a sense this answered a question that I had when reading the texts, namely, could the imagery in an Irish melodrama first produced over 120 years still be emotionally provocative? Clearly in this workshop, the answer was yes, the actors felt the dramatic intensity of that scene work in a visceral way. It also can be read as a silent but powerful critique on the brutality of eviction.

The second portion of the workshop dealt with the relationship between popular theatre, its audiences and the cultural criticism that spoke to the political melodramas in the timeframe. I wished to tie the afternoon's work to a "devised piece [centring on] the rows and debates" about the political melodramas including cultural and theatrical reviews "to highlight the plays' reception and its audiences."[10] To make this work, I took extant reviews and commentary from many voices, including Joseph Holloway, Arthur Griffith, Padraic Colum, *The Irish Times*, the *Evening Herald* and the *New Ireland Review* so as to play with ideas of reception on the other side of representation. By devising 'pieces' that recreated cultural opinion and audience reaction, the actors discussed the potential power of the melodramas playing to large houses, of the differing opinions on popular entertainment in Dublin at the time and of the political tensions driving the country forward towards the Easter Rising. There was a growing awareness of the value of the plays that afternoon; their function as popular theatre and of the rigorous demands made by the form on its players. It also became apparent among the actors that even as they understood the political and social contexts of the timeframe, with experiential and academic knowledge of Irish drama, there were gaps in awareness about Ireland's poor theatre, its histories and its performance aesthetics. Finally, we decided in the workshop itself that we might work some of the war monologues from P. J. Bourke's *When Wexford Rose*, to get a sense of how they might manifest as performance. These were very interesting to play; they were powerful and dramatic as storytelling of the battlefield and of the men and women who fought there. This again opened our eyes to the dramatic potential in some of the works that almost unhooked the melodramatic form for those moments. We had noted this in the first workshop, specifically in *Sarsfield*, but both O'Grady and Bourke's plays perhaps place stronger emphasis on these moments within the form. This second session then established the visual and atmospheric qualities of the plays through the dramatic moments and the tableaux. Uncovering the power of the realistic elements in O'Grady and Bourke as stylistically closer to canonical works was highlighted, as was the emphasis on dramatic moments within the melodramatic form. The session also clearly registered the power of satire when 'pitting' an audience and the physicality and timing required to play out the comic violence for the actors. It also highlighted the agency that the actors, both male and female had to interpret in multiple ways, the fight scenes as comic action in relationship to the audience. The emotive power of the plays and its resonance with modern actors was also made clear. In addition, the actors were coming to understand the plays in their socio-political moments, which layered their understanding of playing the stock. The motifs of nation and class shadowed the scene work, and romance was more or less absent. Finally as I had asked one of the female actors to carry Sadler's speech, I was beginning to consider the dark comic power of the female villain in the patriotic plays as something worthy of deeper investigation.

Workshop Three-Four—October/November 2014

Working with the same group of players in October, this workshop was based on nation and war; I wanted to create that sense of "intensity, sensation and high wire dramatic moments building in emotion through gesture and melodramatic techniques."[11] In parallel to the broad thematic, I wanted to play with melodramatic acting styles in a more structured way. Through my research, I had come across an early Victorian actors' manual by Henry Siddons as "expressive of the various passions, and representing the modern costume of the London Theatres."[12] While I was aware that acting styles progressed with the century, I used the Siddons as a starting point to help the actors understand some melodramatic ways of playing the gamut from comedy all the way to tragedy. Some of the gestures and actions introduced here eventually made their way into the final performance. The warm-ups again included exercises on emotional agility, moving back and forth through states that spoke to melodramatic styles of playing. The morning was given over to rehearsing melodramatic techniques. Drawing from and playing liberally with Siddons' work, I assembled a broad palette of stock gestures depicting different emotional states for the actors. The idea was to create a 'house style' through which to better explore the plays. These expressive gestures were intended to speak to the hero, heroine, villain and the servants. Examples included, for the lower classes, *Servility* (Male) and *Vulgar Triumph* (Female), and for the middle and upper classes, *Pride* (Male), *Tranquil Joy* (Female) and *Horror and Terror* (Female).[13] I also constructed a smaller palette of gestures across class divisions for villainy, including *Conceit, Foppery* and *False Gesture*. I was also not sure of how to represent the abstract notion of nation through gesture, and as it turned out, I used other Siddons' illustrations such as (again) *Pride, Anger* and *Love* to capture the idea. Initially, the actors found ways to use the expressive gestures across an emotional spectrum from the comic to the pathetic to the tragic. As the morning wore on, and the physicality became less stilted, the actors found multiple ways to interpret the expressive gestures, again across the comedy and towards the tragedy. This freed up their initial anxieties around an alien choreography while also opening up the possibilities for the physical score as expression in the plays. In addition, I had specifically wanted to work with expressive gesture for the female villain. After some work shopping the actor kept returning to the 'low' gesture of *Vulgar Triumph* as a darkly comic action that worked best for her as villainous behaviour; the gesture made its way through rehearsals to the final performances. The afternoon was spent attempting to use the techniques in *FTLSL, WWR* and, as additions to the play stock, W.B. Yeats' *The Countess Cathleen (1899)* and Lady Gregory and Yeats' work, *Caitlin ni Houlihan (1902)*. My reason for including two very well-known plays from the Irish canon was that I sensed that melodramatic elements were lurking in their structures. I wanted to test the extent to which these plays sat next to the political melodramas stylistically and to what degree the plays could find crossing points as contemporary performance. The selected scenes for all the plays concentrated on ideas of nation, war and death while trying to adopt or adapt melodramatic playing styles to play out the subject matter. Overall, for *When Wexford Rose* and *For The Land She Loved*, the physical score worked well to underline the melodramatic elements based on nation and war. However, questions did arise as to how much of that choreography was useful in the more realistic moments of Bourke's aesthetics and so how best to clash the different stylistics as a devised work. Again it was noted and discussed how well the plays worked by being aware of the importance of switching emotional states for the actors. When playing with Yeats' and Gregory's work, the actors felt that *The Countess Cathleen* in particular was strong on melodramatic elements depicting women, death and sacrifice particularly, and it was decided that for successive workshops the actors would further investigate the synergies between plays outside the Queen's repertoire and the melodramatic materials. Finally although I did not set out with ideas of class in mind, it became important in this workshop and was clearly revealed to be working in the scripts, specifically *WWR*, sparking discussion on how received notions of Irish class structures in the plays can be interpreted then as now.

The next workshop began with warm-ups that now included playing the Siddons' physical score as well as emotional states, and this became the way in which each warm-up worked. This workshop was to deal with romance and comedy in the plays; I wanted to revisit what had played out in the first workshop, layering what had been since learned of playing comic and tragic tones, to interrogate "melodrama as sex and life and comedy and Nation."[14] I also wanted to explore the nature of sexual violence in the melodramas. Nation would be explored again in detail with Whitbread and Bourke's plays but also with other works, including the nationalist sentiments of Pádraic Pearse *The Singer* (1917) and James Connolly's *Under Which Flag* (1916). I decided on these particular works in much the same vein as selecting the non-melodramatic plays in the previous session. In addition these plays were selected so as to play particularly with the dramatic moments surrounding 1916, the subject matter of which was to form part of the final performancne piece. We were also keen to work with extant verbatim pieces detailing the experience of the 1916 Rising from those on the ground. Finally, we also decided to look at female archetypes, as representation of Irish women's identity on stage, which in this instance included Betsy from *FTLSL*, Cathleen from *The Countess Cathleen* and the Old Woman from *Caitlin ni Houlihan*. A highpoint for the actors was exploring *Sarsfield* through the comedy of romance, sexual innuendo and double meanings in the text. With its major motifs of courtly love mirrored by servant romance, the play works "as an idyll in a way...[yet also playing] with ideas of the ideal to the real,"[15] within the melodramatic storylines. I had intended to clash the romantic scenes up against its more nationalistic tones, as well as play the darker scenes of sexual threat; however, the comedy of courtship alone wore out in the morning. Couples played with love across class, with 'high' and 'low' versions, including the 'sexy landed gentry scenes' and the 'love in the lower orders'; both versions suggested an openness to ways of playing, through the push and pull of wooing. The characters could be suggestive and mocking to one another when playing out the romance, perhaps servant love more so, and their scenes in particular were also more open to the possibility of sex in the playing. That said, the actors all felt that there was much to play with in the scripts around representation of love and of sex through the comedy. Most especially, the women discussed how much more they could play with ideas of love, sex and agency than is immediately accessible when reading the scripts, while the physical style underlined the comedic work. In the afternoon, the tone changed and the women devised a piece, which we called 'the battle of the archetypes' using scripts, physical score and improvisation. The piece involved archetypes of Irish female identity: Betsy, Cathleen and Caitlin as they fight it out with each other for the hearts and minds of the Irish people. We played with this for some time in almost an X Factor way, using melodramatic styles primarily for the sacrificial tones running through the texts. The comedy here, which was strong, came not from the scripts themselves but, ironically, where the straining women pointed up the limits of female representation as archetypal symbols of Ireland. As the most material representation of womanhood, Betsy becomes diminished by the other two archetypal figures. In a way, the workshop itself formed its own story arc. We had begun with Whitbread's comedy of courtship, across class lines and in the melodramatic style. We ended the session with the *Sean-Bhean Bhocht* in *Caitlin ni Houlihan*, a symbolist figure beyond corporeality, a national archetype; as mythmaker, she calls on her sons to sacrifice their lives for Ireland's cause and she is still alive to Irish cultural memory. These stark contrasts marked something for me about female representation, its permissions and its boundaries on the Irish stage. In parallel to the X Factor scenes, the actors were working on the heightened sense of realism in the plays of Pearse and Connelly, which were open to a melodramatic reading at particular moments. However, the character of MacDara in *The Singer* as a male archetype making a maniacal call to blood sacrifice joined to the women's archetypal scene; *MacDara* diminishes all the women in the final moments of the piece, which began a discussion on gender relations on the Irish stage. Finally, playing with verbatim pieces from the 1916 Rising allowed the actors to think about the relationship between the theatrical moment and its historical mirror on the streets of Dublin. We played with the idea of Watchmen as projected beginning for the performance piece, significantly this began our thinking on an everyman/everywoman character to carry the story making for an audience. We left this open for investigation in the coming sessions.

5.3   Outcomes

1. To better understand the ways in which the political melodramas functioned as performance

As discussed previously, there exists anxiety when Irish stereotypes are in question, which can overemphasise its playing for comic effect or as ironic device. Considering the long history of negative and reductive stereotypes employed to portray the Irish by others, which have, as is well documented, been both internalised and cast out, that is a realistic expectation.[16] When working with the plays, that worry remained for a time and was complicated by the fact that a large number of the scripts were written (Whitbread aside) by Irish people. That makes the enquiry so much more complex to deal with. Bearing in mind the sheer drop of historical weight, the workshop process had to bring the stereotype into the open in an immediate way. As discussed, what was established quite quickly was that the plays *worked* (to various degrees) far better 'up on their feet' as performance than was expected by everyone, including myself. That initial and principal discovery allowed feelings of nervousness to dissipate about the stereotype along with some lack of faith that the plays could speak on their own terms. Accepting the stereotype on this level freed the actors to begin *playing* with the scripts, unlocking their melodramatic form; their recurring motifs of romance, nation and class; their theatrical devices and use of language; their visual imagery and physicality; their realistic impulse and their comic and tragic switches. Playing the scenes through the workshop processes revealed the comic and dramatic structures of the works and discovered how integral the melodramatic aesthetic of emotional switching was to their performance. Playing the switches between comedy and drama revealed the comic convention of the double act as performance— its signalling of love and ambiguity through romance, and of *knowing better* in the defeat of the British through class and nation. As the workshops progressed, understanding the nature and function of visual imagery, atmospherics and tableaux became central to our understanding of melodramatic dramaturgy. This came with a growing awareness of the importance of the physical score, vital to understanding the playing of the aesthetic and leading on to the actors' developing *ways of playing* that aesthetic. A sense of agency for the comic women also revealed itself through the weeks, under the same motifs and along the spectrum of the aesthetic expressive elements. It became clear that *totality of expression* as political melodrama would have impacted powerfully on its audiences. Those explorations as extra-textual analysis created a series of exploratory practice-as-research paths to journey down in search of the nature and function of the patriotic plays, forming the spine of the workshop period, embedded in the rehearsal stages in the following year and deeply rooted by the final performances.

2. To better understand elements of melodramatic form by creating a physical score with resonance to contemporary aesthetics

As the process moved forward, it became evident that melodramatic playing often felt alien to actors who are trained to a more realistic style. Using Siddons' manual as a point of departure allowed the actors a means to deepen their awareness of playing melodrama. Creating a physical score in practice helped the actors to extend their understanding of playing stock characters, giving them a scaffold on which to build their performances. That scaffolding also acted as a key; once comfortable with the structure of the physical score as support to the playing, the actors were able to improvise ways of performing the scene work. That practical knowledge opened the script up to interpretation and ways of playing for the actors in relationship with an audience. Large portions of the early rehearsal schedule for production were dedicated to working in this way in order to create a 'house' style for the actors to call up and use, including stock gestures and actions to signify, the hero, the heroine, the servant and the villain and for stage pictures or tableaux. For production, the company created a scale for the physical score, so that stock expressive gesture worked across major to minor keys depending on what the scenes required. While the tableaux or stage pictures almost always worked in the major keys, the scale allowed the actors some freedom when moving from more realistic moments to a more melodramatic style. Gaining such practical knowledge illuminates the theoretical insights into melodramatic styles, layering the actors' understanding of the dynamics, potential and demands of performance. It also demonstrates the relationship between the structures of the resonant style that we created based on historicised ideas of the aesthetic as it acts as a key to unlock the texts for the actors. The intention was never to recreate verisimilitude in any mimetic sense but to resonate with the contemporary aesthetic. That devising of a physical score in workshop gave a way in to play the form. Significantly, those interventions opened the texts to their porous edges for the actors, giving confidence to work with the form and allowing for multiple interpretations and ways of playing for the actors in relationship with the audience. This way of playing integrally informed the final performances; this knowing-in-doing would be difficult to access by other means of enquiry alone.

3. To better understand elements of melodramatic form by focussing on the aesthetic of 'emotional switching' in the patriotic plays

If understanding how a physical score works to scaffold a melodramatic aesthetic, the same can be said for 'emotional switching': what that might ask of the actor and what that might mean when trying to know how the form functions. Switching emotionally from lighter or comic scenes to dramatic or tragic tones is deeply embedded into the melodramatic way of playing as a central stylistic. Not unlike the physical demands, this way of emoting, which is underscored by sincerity and intensity of feeling, was difficult for the actors to come to grips with. The fact that emotional switching could also accommodate realistic moments under the arch of the melodramatic sign as it assimilated differing formal elements was also challenging. The workshops became laboratory spaces at times, so as to understand how that 'switching' worked in practice. Grasping its mechanics played out through the rehearsal period ensured that emotional switching became a central aesthetic in the final performances. Working the technique informed the playing in a number of ways. It deepened the actors' understanding of how best to play with the motifs of romance, nation and class. Becoming aware of how to 'emote' informed the actors' understanding of how the comic, tragic and realistic elements paced and flowed through the form. Significantly, realising the mechanics of legibility through the emotive aesthetic as sign system for an audience, also freed the actors to read between the lines through which the subtext could flow. As with the physical languages of melodrama, the emotive *switch* can act as a key to utterance, suggestion and nuance, which again opens the scripts to other possibilities for playing and seeing. Working with the emotive stylistic again indicates theoretical understanding of the form. Importantly, it reveals how performance possibilities may have worked for the contemporary actor in a way that is not as visible when dealing with the text alone.

4. To consider comic conventions as practice within the melodramatic form towards an emphasis on comic women

In tandem with the actors' grasping the demands of the melodramatic style, the comic structures started to work at deeper levels. Perhaps ironically and as already noted, early tendencies were to play the stock characters for comedy alone. Working for audience laughter is an enticing trap when playing stock character; this is not to say that its use is not necessary, rather than playing only for laughs pulls from the richness of the melodramatic aesthetic. Understanding how the form functions means that the players could perform without getting caught solely in that particular comic expectation. By unhooking the cliché, by allowing the work its own terms and building on the performance knowledge learned, the actors were able to play in multiple ways within the plays' comic structures. The comedy of cross-class courtship was immediately visible and returned to on a number of occasions through the workshop processes. Working as doubles revealed the romantic comedy occurring between both 'high' and 'low' couples although the servants' comedy of faux aggressive courtship was much more developed. With the physical score and emotional switch as scaffold, the actors growing confidence was brought to bear on the text and subtext in the works over time. They played easily, even joyfully, with the servants' romance, with its misunderstandings, its pseudo mockery, its double meanings and with the women's deferrals of marriage. While the stock characters of hero and heroine also worked within the same broad aesthetic and there was some mirroring, the servants carry the comic weight, although I suspect there is room to explore the hero-heroine stock as comic performance in more depth. That said, they don't conventionally work as wilfully under the comic sign and can, at times, be more laughed at than with. The actors also played with darker, satirical or more absurd comic strains along with comic violence at work in the plays. As with courtship the comedy of class contains lighter and darker comic moments and is performed by the servants in repeating patterns, connecting to the idea of saving the masters in defeat of the British. The power of slapstick played out in the action scenes and in the tableaux, with the discovery that the women also had strong agency to threaten or commit comic violence. In addition, the stage directions clearly opened up the performance possibilities for creating alternative narratives with an audience. The villain's playing, with its dark satirical tones, is also open to the actor's power to interpret and manipulate the audience to passionate feelings of pleasurable hatred. Using the physical and emotive score, the female villain's use of direct address to the audience revealed the powerful nature of the stereotype. In all then, understanding the comic patterns described and not falling into the trap of the cliché allow the actors, both male and female, to play liberally with text and subtext, creating layers of possible intention in relationship with the audience. All of these comic processes made their way into rehearsal and the final performances. The workshop approach allowed the actors the space and time to experiment with comic composition and revealed the extent to which the comic men and women are at work in the patriotic plays. In my view, that comes through understanding how the material and comic material worked in practice, which reveals their possible *ways of playing* and so enriches the written accounts and textual analysis of the previous chapters. On many levels the practice as research lens, worked through these pages and the years of the project, that *knowing in doing* reveals in a very real way the performance possibilities for the political melodramas. And with that comes the idea of multiple ways of communicating with an audience that moves beyond the text alone. That opens up the landscape of meaning making as theatre. That landscape looks into the gaping maw that is the study of comic women in Irish popular theatre. An academic approach alone would not have brought the same series of rich, deep performative realisations about the comic woman in the plays. The knowledge gained through the practical work, understanding the power of agency with which comic woman can work, through the structures and approaches described, is alive in practice, giving strength and support to the work of the previous chapters. Further, I believe that the comic woman has been obscured in large part by the dominant figure of her male counterpart in theatre histories. A research-as-practice lens deepens the revelation of that hidden history here fusing fast, in my view to the way of the comic everywoman, and the final performance piece, to the story of Marian and Joseph.

5.4   Marian and Joseph

At the end of the initial workshop process, I began to create a devised and scripted piece of work for production. I wanted to create a performance piece built from the knowledge gained in the workshops and for a general audience. The piece would interrogate ideas of romance, nation and class at work in the patriotic plays, orbiting the 1916 Rising.[17] What emerged was a work much inspired by Ariane Mnouchkine's *1789* called 'Mise' which translates from Irish as 'Me' or 'I.'[18] *Mise* met with a lukewarm response from the actors; they felt (ironically) that the piece was too large and convoluted in plot and scope. In August 2015 I ran four two-hour refresher sessions with the actors, focussing again on romance, nation and class, concentrating on stock physical and emotive language, with emphasis on female agency through comic and tragic moments across the patriotic and literary plays. Over Christmas, I wrote the initial scene work for what would become *Marian and Joseph: A Revolutionary Love Story.* In early 2016 and with two actors, I began to rehearse initial scenes from the piece, written in an episodic style, which staged as a performance installation as part of Proclamation Day celebrations. The production notes described the work as "combining performance and archival film … looking through the … eyes [of] the noted diarist Joseph Holloway and the Sligo actress Marian Culler [the work]…interrogates popular theatre as that with the power to voice … aspirations to national identity."[19]

Joseph Holloway was in fact of the real world, a contemporary critic and an architect who designed the first Abbey Theatre for W.B. Yeats.[20] Joseph was written not as an Everyman character, but as a chronicler of the period, who was as comfortable in the Queen's as the Abbey and his writing describes their histories unfolding through real time. I thought him an interesting construct as character that could cross poor poetics and literary aesthetics easily, as an upper middle class man in love with the popular theatre actress Marian Culler. Marian was drawn as a fictitious working-class woman who came to Dublin from the West, to work as an actress for Mr Bourke at the Queen's. The story of their brief but ultimately doomed courtship was to become central to the finished piece.[21] I wrote the remainder of Marian and Joseph as a first draft in time for rehearsals in the summer of 2016, with three performances scheduled for November, two in Sligo and one in Dublin. Most if not all were familiar with the premise for the work, and as additional support, I brought in a movement coach to create a physical and stylised language that underpinned the melodramatic stylistic. I also brought in a set designer and producer who worked closely with us during the rehearsal period through to production. The rehearsal process solidified what had been sketched in the workshops, lasting three months and resulting in the final piece, as non-linear and episodic theatre.

Marian and Joseph attempted to capture the tensions of the time leading up the 1916 Rising along with the stylistics and power of popular theatre for its audiences. The press release, which echoes the earlier installation, described the piece:

> *Marian and Joseph: A Revolutionary Love Story* is an episodic piece which attempts to capture the spirit of Irish Political Melodrama performed at the Queen's Theatre ... Looking through the lens of Marian and Joseph's relationship, the play examines Irish 'poor' theatre, which voiced popular aspirations to national identity through some of the most ... formative years in Irish history. This is their story.

As extracts many of the melodramatic plays were integral to the performance text including *Lord Edward, Wolfe Tone, Sarsfield, When Wexford Rose, For The Land She Loved* along with *The Countess Cathleen, Caitlin ni Houlihan* and *The Singer*. Included too were Holloway's (and others) reviews and accounts of the political melodramas at the Queen's and the Abbey plays, his journal entries on the nature of art and the actor and some 1916 verbatim pieces. Many of the extracts were played for comic effect from broad to black, but they were also played for dramatic moments; Marian and Joseph's characters were realistic portrayals acting as the connective thread through the episodic structure of the play. Their courtship was something that an audience could empathise with, coming from different class systems, they both fully inhabited the theatre world and they both had deep though different responses to the turmoil of the Rising. Onto their story I hooked the stylistics of the patriotic plays and I built a chorus of Queen's actors to carry elements of the narrative. The central idea was to showcase poor theatre and to reflect the political and social tensions that the plays were born of. Added to that and built from the workshops the script and the rehearsals came the principal motif of women of the popular stage. The character of Marian encapsulated a dual function for the play. The audience witness her as 'actress' working at the Queen's and playing, as bricolage, all the female roles of the patriotic melodramas; heroine, servant and villain, and working in the main under the comic sign. She also played her everyday 'self,' an Irish working-class woman navigating her own journey through love and war. In many respects Marian became a cipher for the comic everywoman as actress playing out the principal comic roles and as a material everyday woman finding her way through her world. This then formed the spine of the play through which were channelled the same signals and motifs that traced through the workshops, devising and rehearsal processes. The final theatre piece while very close to the research in many respects is answering a different set of expectations as performance. However, the workshop processes built the theatre piece, which did not move very far from the knowing-in-doing that came from the initial exploratory sessions. Marian began in the workshops and developed through the rehearsal process; her subjectivity was central to the play. Although not born of the earlier processes, she is grown from them and in that sense she embodies that connection as performative *clew* between the comic everywoman and her everyday self in this final discussion.

5.5   The Comic Everywoman

Sos Eltis' objective is to make visible the theatrical, conventional and conceptual apparatus as meaning maker with contemporary audiences, shining a light into some dark theatre and performance histories for women. My work incorporates the same desire. The contingencies of the contemporary moment, the mechanics of the melodramatic form, its place in Irish theatre histories, the gendered comic analyses of undervalued popular texts and exploratory practice all speak to that desire. Comic women sit at the heart of that discussion. For me, the comic everywoman represents the possibility for speaking to her contemporary audience in ways other than that which is already known. Understanding the workings of the form and its comic potential roots and grows that thinking. Placing women on popular stages as the century waxes and wanes must account for the social and formal relations in which she is materially embedded. Those realities begin to offer the 'twisting of the sense' I spoke about, as alternate ways of seeing the performing comic woman on the popular stage. Exploring ways of playing, as expressive tools through which to communicate with an audience, opens up possibilities for understanding how the comic everywoman played. Expressive tools with which to communicate the lattice of readable signs as a totality of comic expression with the audience. These ideas shape the comic everywoman as familiar female identity on the patriotic stage within a bank of theatrical knowledge and innovation and within a matrix of understanding between audience and players. She is located in the tradition, culture and popularity of nationalist plays in the city and along the theatrical axis by the turn of the late nineteenth century. That comic cognito describes her worth. She orchestrates misunderstanding, obfuscates institutional recuperation, upsets status and collapses class; she can draw comic blood and play with sexual threat. She can be the enemy, bring up bile and enjoy her downfall. She is discordant at the limits of her representation. For me that signals levels of agency for comic women that have been hidden, and for me that signals ways in which to *play* with that agency in her performance moment, transmitting out, speaking out to her contemporary counterpart. Yet, and in many respects this study represents a beginning, it is a sketch distilled through the formula of the comic everywoman, a way in to try and understand how comic identity worked for women on popular stages in Ireland. There is much more to be done.

Robert K. Sarlos argues for an approach to theatre histories "that is within the scholar's reach—sometimes working *as* artists, sometimes *with* them—to deepen the artist's and spectator's understanding of ... theatrical golden age[s]".[22] Sarlos argues for a performance reconstruction (within an environmental one) as that which "bring[s] participants ... closer to a sensory realization of the style and atmosphere, the physical and emotional dynamics of a bygone era, than mere reading can."[23] Broadly, this is what I set out to do throughout the years that have encapsulated the entirety of this academic and practice enquiry. That journey began with wanting to understand how Irish political melodramas functioned as performance, with increasing centrality to comic performance and then to comic women in performance. I wanted to investigate if a deeper understanding of poor theatre and comic women could be important to the field of knowledge in Irish theatre histories, female theatre histories and performance studies. The final performances did in certain respects reconstruct elements of the patriotic melodramas through scene work and physical action scenes and importantly through experimentation with ways of playing as resonant rather than mimetic representation. The approach attempted to mediate the *presentist* trap, allowing distant dramatic texts to live on their own terms and attempting to avoid a modern interpretation to shadow or warp the reading of the texts. Acknowledging the difficulties inherent in reconstruction of an 'original' arguably, when the work is speaking from within its own terms, new insights are available. Tracey Davis' argument is useful here; she believes that a feminist revisionist approach as a theatre historian brings fundamental questions with it:

> If feminist historians are going to rewrite history, the revisions must cut deeply ... greater attention to period-based histories of women's lives and culture would undoubtedly enhance most theatre research in contemporary and distant eras and may inspire researchers to locate and tap unusual types of evidence.[24]

This study tries in its totality to reach that discussion within a feminist revisionist approach; to interrogate female comic identity on Irish popular stages, locating her and connecting her as performative *clew* to her life, to her culture, to her everyday 'self.' That attempt argues for a revisioning of Irish theatre to incorporate female comic performance histories that sit outside the canon and a feminist revisionist perspective, which centres on the relationship between performance and cultural text. There is much more to be done here, but the comic everywoman, grounded by the material reality of the conditions of production and reception, can act as that performative *clew*, can as Susan Carlson suggests act as a model for real women, can embody and connect to that relationship, and can connect to her everyday 'self' beyond the theatre walls, in the material world. Following the thread through the dark arrives at a lack. That lack must be filled with a greater understanding of women's lives and culture on the other side of the performative act. As a future act, tying the thread to a deeper understanding of that reciprocity must be the next step.

To go back for a moment at the end, as part of the earlier workshops, I explored the connections between the popular plays and at times more established or valued pieces of theatre work. Out of that came the idea for the last scene in the performance piece. In this scene and in a dream, Marian meets with the Countess Cathleen and Caitlin ni Houlihan. There she vies with them for Joseph's love, but ultimately she is disappeared from the stage by the archetypal women, who themselves are in turn diminished by the male sacrificial hero. The scene works to message the disappearance of the material woman as *less than* other representations, *less than* the idealisations of Irish womanhood. In a very real sense her 'self' within the tradition of popular theatre is also reflected as *less than* other representations in Irish theatre histories. Cathy Leeney argues that it is "profoundly misleading to judge old plays by old reviews … nor can we deem such plays unworthy of production if they were deemed unworthy in the past."[25] While Leeney is speaking to the tensions for women writers in the period, the point stands for women performers in the popular theatre. The representation and reception of comic women on those stages were deemed unworthy and by a host of voices. Melissa Sihra furthers the point when she discusses the fact that feminist scholars are beginning to interrogate hidden or forgotten texts. The project must attempt to pluralise Irish theatre histories and excavate the value judgements that constitute the canon. Sihra points to the value of recovery by situating the works in its conditions of production that necessarily includes but moves outside the text alone to its ideological, historical, cultural, gendered and embodied moments. Sihra rightly argues also for caution, that celebratory poetics will not serve, that "inequality should not obscure quality."[26] The word quality is a sticky subject and in the end circles back to what I have discussed in this book.

NOTES

1. The timing was good. Ireland's *Decade of Centenaries* had recently come into being; its remit includes ways to commemorate and interrogate 'significant events' in Irish history between 1912 and 1922. Dublin City Council's *Citizens in Conflict* centenary programme primarily funded the project, which was well received.
2. Workshop One, Journal Notes 24.06.14.
3. Workshop One, Journal Notes 24.06.14.
4. Workshop One, Journal Notes 24.06.14.
5. Workshop One, Journal Notes 24.06.14.
6. Workshop One, Journal Notes 24.06.14.
7. Workshop Two, Journal Notes, 19.07.14.
8. Workshop Two, Journal Notes, 19.07.14.
9. See Christopher Fitz-Simon, *Buffoonery and Easy Sentiment: Popular Irish Plays in the Decade Prior to the Opening of the Abbey Theatre* (Dublin: Carysfort Press, 2011), pp. 80–84.
10. Workshop Two, Journal Notes, 19.07.14.
11. Workshop Three, Journal Notes, Oct/Nov 2014.
12. Henry Siddons, *Practical Illustration of Rhetorical Gesture and Action; adapted to the English Drama; From a work on the subject by M. Engel, member of the royal academy of Berlin* (1822).
13. Henry Siddons, *Practical Illustration of Rhetorical Gesture and Action.*
14. Fourth workshop frame for building ensemble, Nov 2014.
15. Notes to Workshop Four Oct/Nov 2014.
16. See Micheál Ó hAodha, *"Insubordinate Irish,"* Travellers in the Text (Manchester: Manchester University Press, 2011); Colin Graham, *Deconstructing Ireland; Identity, Theory Culture* (Edinburgh, Edinburgh University Press, 2001); Christopher Morash, *A History of Irish Theatre;* Stephen Watt, *Joyce, O'Casey and the Irish Popular Theatre* (New York: Syracuse University Press, 1991).
17. I intended to apply for funding from the state that had funding streams available for the commemorations in order to mount the production.
18. In the funding application to the Irish Arts Council in 2015, I described the work broadly as "A multi-dimensional promenade … theatre piece …

Two central characters will immerse the audience ... as interrogation of forgotten working-class melodramatic expressions of nationalism, to the 1916 Rising streets and beyond", Arts Council Application 2015.

19. Production Notes—Proclamation Day, March 2015.

20. On his death the family estate donated a vast amount of materials to the National Library. As such his accounts, reviews and playbills constitute not only a valuable source for research but are as close an account of the period as it's possible to find.

21. The performance on Proclamation Day itself worked as an installation; there was a visual and audio landscape playing as a silent third character to Marian and Joseph's scene work. That scenography comprised of recruitment posters in Ireland for First World War, film of Irish regiments in First World War and film of Easter Week that I had gotten the rights to from the Imperial War Museum. There were Queen's Theatre playbills (some from Easter Week); early Irish cinema, which were the political melodramas transposed onto films, and some imagery of Joseph Holloway, the Abbey and The Countess Cathleen. Some of this scenography was also used in the full-length production later in the year.

22. Robert K. Sarlos, cited in Gilli Bush-Bailey, 'Putting it into Practice: The possibilities and problems of practical research for the theatre historian', in *Contemporary Theatre Review*, https://doi.org/10.1080/1086800208568697, p. 81.

23. Robert K. Sarlos, cited in Gilli Bush-Bailey, 'Putting it into Practice: The possibilities and problems of practical research for the theatre historian', p. 81.

24. Tracey Davis, cited in Gilli Bush-Bailey, 'Putting it into Practice: The possibilities and problems of practical research for the theatre historian', p. 80.

25. Cathy Leeney quoted in *Women in Irish Drama*, Ed. by Melissa Sihra (Palgrave: Basingstoke, 2007), p. 10.

26. Edna Longley quoted in *Women in Irish Drama*, Ed. by Melissa Sihra, p. 11.

BIBLIOGRAPHY

Bailey, Gilli Bush. Putting It into Practice: The Possibilities and Problems of Practical Research for the Theatre Historian. *Contemporary Theatre Review*. https://doi.org/10.1080/1086800208568697.

Eltis, Sos. 2013. *Acts of Desire: Women and Sex on Stage 1800–1930*. Oxford: Oxford University Press.

Fitz-Simon, Christopher. 2011. *Buffoonery and Easy Sentiment: Popular Irish Plays in the Decade Prior to the Opening of the Abbey Theatre*. Dublin: Carysfort Press.

For the Land They Loved: Irish Political Melodramas 1890–1925, ed. Cheryl Herr (Syracuse: Syracuse University Press, 1991).

Graham, Colin. 2001. *Deconstructing Ireland; Identity, Theory Culture*. Edinburgh: Edinburgh University Press.

Morash, Christopher. 2002. *A History of Irish Theatre, 1601–2000*. Cambridge: Cambridge University Press.

Ó hAodha, Micheál. 2011. *"Insubordinate Irish," Travellers in the Text*. Manchester: Manchester University Press.

Siddons, Henry. 1822. *Practical Illustration of Rhetorical Gesture and Action; Adapted to the English Drama; From a Work on the Subject by M. Engel, Member of the Royal Academy of Berlin*.

Watt, Stephen. 1991. *Joyce, O'Casey and the Irish Popular Theatre*. New York: Syracuse University Press.

Women in Irish Drama, ed. Melissa Sihra (Palgrave: Basingstoke, 2007).

CHAPTER 6

Close In

Abstract The Close In signals back to the social, political and cultural contexts within which the political plays are embedded and to the Queen's Theatre in Dublin, which represented the heart of the matter. It briefly recaps that particular brand of popular nationalist theatre as underrated for many in the cultural arena, which continues as a lineage of anxiety. My consideration here suggests that the patriotic plays while stamped with the nationalist emblem as popular theatre can be read in differing ways. That alternative history tells the story of the comic everywoman on the Irish popular stage—her comic agency and subversion as transitory power in that space and as connective *clew* to her counterpart in everyday experience. The comic everywoman is transmitting to be seen and heard, if only we would let her.

Keywords Political • Melodrama • Popular • Theatre • Comedy • Comic Everywoman

I found the political melodramas while researching Irish music hall a number of years ago. I was instantly hooked by the prospect of studying the native dramas as popular or poor theatre in Ireland. I knew from my research into Irish comedy that popular theatre is underrated in its performance histories and criticism. Working from those few who have walked

© The Author(s) 2018
S. Colleary, *The Comic Everywoman in Irish Popular Theatre*,
Palgrave Studies in Comedy,
https://doi.org/10.1007/978-3-030-02008-8_6

the path before me, I began by looking into the socio-historical contexts in relationship to the poor plays and their playwrights. I also began researching the Queen's Theatre in Dublin, known by some (and not by others) as the 'House of Irish Drama.' That house stood as ground zero for the patriotic plays and grew an audience with a spirit of popular nationalism. Amongst differing and oppositional cultural politics, poor theatre made its own brand within the competing factions and changing faces of nationalism on Dublin stages. Criticism has been various and the overriding terms of the discussion are centred not surprisingly on poor theatre's politics. Notwithstanding the scholarship the sense persists that the Queen's brand of political theatre is *less* rather than other; that is, of less value than the emergent separatist, cultural and political movements during the period. In certain respects the melodramatic form itself takes the brunt of the criticism. Worn out, outdated, unable to speak to a changing society, cheap entertainment for the masses, with no real political agenda and no appetite for change. Damned with faint praise phraseology; 'good for morale' and little else, embedded in the 'blarney and blather' of a British melodramatic theatrical tradition. A theatrical tradition so very out of place with those moving towards separatism in a post-Parnellite society, where its popularity was no excuse. Perhaps some of that judgement is bound to proximity anxiety between London and Dublin as the second city of the Empire. Cleaving away from the notion was crucial in some quarters and fed the cultural anxiety around a form that sat so close to the British aesthetic. Perhaps too, that lineage of anxiety lived on into the newly minted state and on again to its residuals.

To criticise the political melodramas for that which they were not, and for that which they could not be, to my mind, misses the point. This study then looks to what the political melodramas *did* do, as performance texts emblazoned with nationalist political sentiment, working through the demands of the melodramatic aesthetic writ large for popular audiences. As mass entertainment the patriotic plays worked their dramaturgies switching out tragic and comic motifs side by side. Understanding those structures reveals how the comedy worked and how comic women worked in the plays. Those structures give up their secrets of subversion and reversion for comic women in the inverted theatre space. The construction of the comic everywoman belongs here. She represents comic possibility in the space. The comic everywoman on Irish popular stages is grounded within her cultural, political and performance moment. She is a familiarised female comic identity within a bank of theatrical knowledge and innovation and in a matrix of understanding with her audience. The comic everywoman has the totality of expressive means to perform acts of communication with her audience. Her comic cognito as expression, as performative *clew*, transmits out to her everyday self. In that performative ambivalent potential moment, she speaks of class, she speaks of gender, she speaks of nation; with transitory comic agency and through the totality of legible signs she expresses those restrictive cultural and theatrical perceptions and coda that seek to constrain and recuperate her. This work can only sketch that idea here. She represents a poetic, a beginning only, she is a key, a way in to understanding comic women on popular stages in Ireland in relationship with her audience and her everyday world. Of necessity, the scale of this work can only take her this far. There is much to be done: to my mind, comic women in popular theatre are hidden in Irish performance histories. We must recover those women, those stories, those performance histories. What I have drawn out in this work requires further archival research, research practice and academic study. In addition, there is much room to interrogate patriarchal power relations and women's sexuality on popular stages in Ireland, as well as the dangerous women of popular theatre. There is also much room to interrogate for gender in the double act and with it comic violence and women on stage. It is very difficult for women to appear if they are caught in historical, formal and cultural amnesia. It is difficult for women to appear if they are caught by traditional comic convention and in danger of the looming status quo on the horizon. It is very difficult for women to appear against the tide of powerful patriarchal and cultural forces that haunt the past and ghost the present, those who influence decision-making on what has and what has *not* value. In the last moment here, I am borrowing from Gilli Bush-Bailey who uses Virginia Woolf to make the point for feminist theatre historians, "we cannot understand the present if we isolate it from the past …. We must become the people that we were two or three generations ago. Let us be our great grandmothers."[1] I spoke recently of women's comic voices as the "struggle to be heard, a condition of malaise that has debilitated, misshapen or threatened to extinguish the very sound."[2] This book represents another challenge to make that heard.

NOTES

1. Virginia Woolf quoted in Gilli Bush-Bailey, *Putting it into Practice*, p. 92.
2. Susanne Colleary, *Performance and Identity in Irish Stand-Up Comedy: The Comic 'i'* (Hampshire: Palgrave, 2015).

BIBLIOGRAPHY

Colleary, Susanne. 2015. *Performance and Identity in Irish Stand-Up Comedy: The Comic 'i'*. Hampshire: Palgrave.

SCENE NINE—THE NEW PLAY

Note to Scene Nine

In the construction of the unpublished play script, of which Scene Nine is part, several sources were utilised and in several different ways. At times those sources were quoted, at other times they were partially used in the construction of character dialogue, and sometimes they were paraphrased. Those sources then helped to construct the scene here as bricolage. I have tried to fully record their uses as part of a working actor's script. In that sense the format while unusual, is fully intent on capturing those sources as used in the script and as the notes and the references evidence.

VX—*New Play poster as backdrop*—**THE CLUICHE CAOINTE.**[1] *LX slowly fade up to reveal* **JOSEPH** *upstage left in the shadow of the VX.* **JOSEPH's** *house is also in shadow. Enter* **MARIAN** *from downstage right dressed in the same outfit as when we first met her. They see and move directly towards each other.*

JOSEPH (*a more confident* **JOSEPH** *than we have seen before*)
There's a new play at the … (*He looks at his notes*)
I note the ….. (*He trails off, then directly to* **MARIAN**)
Are you rehearsing?

© The Author(s) 2018
S. Colleary, *The Comic Everywoman in Irish Popular Theatre,*
Palgrave Studies in Comedy,
https://doi.org/10.1007/978-3-030-02008-8

MARIAN   No.

JOSEPH (*offers Marian his hand*)
    Marian?

MARIAN (*she puts her hand in his as she responds*)
    Yes?

JOSEPH   Did you love me?

MARIAN   I'm not certain

JOSEPH   Of what my love?

SX of Riverstown fiddler Michael Coleman's Mrs Kelly's Waltz begins on **MARIAN**'s *reply and* **JOSEPH** *pulls* **MARIAN** *close. The scratchy fiddle stays low to begin with, and they take some steps of a waltz together in a slow circle about the central playing area.*

MARIAN (*happy*)   Oh! This waltz!

They continue to dance slowly for a few moments. They are held in a quiet joy to be in each other's company. After some moments, enter **ACTOR THREE** *upstage right as* **The Countess Cathleen**. *She comes downstage right; she has a graceful and birdlike movement, ruffling her feathers as if to shake something off, this is a rhythm that she keeps as she moves; when she speaks, she is still, taking on a soft pose that has the bearing of a high priestess. She begins to speak.* **JOSEPH** *sees* **The Countess Cathleen** *and feels drawn to her. He looks into* **MARIAN**'s *face as they continue to dance in a wide circle at the edge of the central playing area.*

I loved you (*softly*)

The Countess Cathleen   I am the Countess Cathleen

JOSEPH *stops dancing and looks at* **The Countess Cathleen**. **MARIAN** *continues dancing as if* **JOSEPH** *were still leading her in the circle; she seems doll-like and expressionless. For the moment she does not react to the action. The fiddle playing continues throughout.*

JOSEPH (*enthralled by the presence of* **The Countess Cathleen,** *and it tells in his voice*)
"I watch enraptured as if I were in fairyland..."

The Countess Cathleen
I save the starving peasants from selling their souls
In exchange for bread (*begins moving further downstage, continuing her birdlike rhythm*)

JOSEPH (*follows her with the turn of his body but does not move*)
"The merchant-demons trafficking in the immortal souls of the poor starving peasants"

The Countess Cathleen
(*stopping and taking up her soft pose*)
"Oh that so many pitchers of rough clay
Should prosper and the porcelain break in two"

JOSEPH (*reaches towards her and takes a step*)
"Until the beautiful self-sacrificing Countess..."

The Countess Cathleen
(*moving downstage further and cutting across Joseph, her pitch and tone rising in intensity*)
"Lay all the bags in a heap
And when I am gone..." (**The Countess Cathleen** *comes downstage centre right*)

JOSEPH (*intense and excited, the pace becomes faster, and the lines come almost on top of one another*)
"Share them out...
To every man and woman"[2]

JOSEPH   "To be awarded a crown of glory for so supreme a sacrifice!"[3]

MARIAN *has danced in the circle throughout this piece and is now near* **JOSEPH** *again. He steps into her rhythm and begins to dance in the same arc with her again.* **The Countess Cathleen** *holds her soft pose and remains.*

From time to time she repeats her birdlike ruffling of feathers and actions through the scene, but remains silent.

MARIAN (*afraid, but distant somehow*)
"Hold me tightly [Joseph]
...for the storm
Is dragging me away...."[4]
JOSEPH *returns his full attention to* **MARIAN**, *and they dance again, in their way about the circle, moving away from the figure of* **The Countess Cathleen**. *There is another moment of joy held between them.*

JOSEPH (*with some love and distress*)

I loved you...

As he says this, enter **ACTOR FOUR** *as the* **Old Woman** *from upstage left. She also moves in her rhythm, she forms a cruciform as she moves and speaks when she is still, she is powerful and strident and dark.* **JOSEPH** *slows the dance and, leaving* **MARIAN**, *moves towards the sight.* **MARIAN** *continues the dance on her own for some moments only before she becomes aware of the* **Old Woman**. *She stops slowly and steps away from the dance. This is occurring as* **JOSEPH** *turns towards the sight of the* **Old Woman** *who travels in stages downstage left, stopping as she speaks.*

Old Woman   "It's a hard service they take that help me.
Many that are red-cheeked now will be pale-cheeked"

MARIAN *cuts across these lines. She tries to hold on to* **JOSEPH**. *He is again enraptured and follows the* **Old Woman** *despite* **MARIAN's** *protests; he seems not to notice* **MARIAN**. *It suddenly feels like a battleground.*

MARIAN   Joseph! (*The* **Old Woman** *continues moving downstage centre; she stops*)

"Many that have been free to walk the hills and the bogs and the rushes,
Will be sent to walk hard streets in far countries"

JOSEPH (*moving closer to her*)

"I am thrilled by her weird beauty"

MARIAN   No! No! Joseph

The **Old Woman** *moves quickly now, downstage centre. She breaks her pattern, speaking as she walks. She sees* **The Countess Cathleen**, *and stops opposite her, yet facing out. She becomes more powerful as she speaks to the audience.*

"They that had red cheeks will have pale cheeks for my sake;"
"And for all that…"

JOSEPH (*overlapping her*)
"Her words sunk into one's very soul!"

MARIAN (*distressed, attempting to pull* **JOSEPH** *away, and moving
      towards each woman as she tries to stop what is happening*)
      Joseph! You love me! Don't you remember!

(*She rages at both the* **Old Woman** *and* **The Countess Cathleen**)

Ya oul Whore! (*to the* **Old Woman**)

Ya oul Bitch! (*to* **The Countess Cathleen**)

The **Old Woman** *and* **The Countess Cathleen** *begin to renew their chants simultaneously and their movement rhythms almost as if competition, yet they do not acknowledge each other; they maintain their distance and separate power.* **MARIAN** *is in distress, she knows she is in danger, but she does not fully understand why, there is a feeling of chaos during these moments.*

Old Woman (*with pitch and intensity, this is the call to war*)

"They shall be remembered forever.
They shall be alive forever."

The Countess Cathleen (*with rising yet quiet power, these lines are to be spoken across each other but still to be heard*)

"Oh that so many pitchers of rough clay
Should prosper and the porcelain break in two"

JOSEPH (*enraptured*)
"A painful joy enveloped my senses…"

Old Woman   "They shall be speaking forever
The people shall hear them forever"[5]

The Countess Cathleen
"…Lay all the bags… When I am gone……. Share them out…
To every man and woman"[6]

JOSEPH (*sublime*)
"…and left me in an ecstasy of misery that was good to feel!"[7]

MARIAN *confronts* JOSEPH

MARIAN   I know our hearts were true, and that our arms were strong… Am I dying for my country, Joseph?

JOSEPH (*returns to her with deep anger and hurt*)

You never loved me!

JOSEPH *kisses* MARIAN *on the mouth. It is a kiss with anger and hurt wrapped up in it. He pushes her face into his shoulder as he tries to silence her. She struggles and cries and then becomes still. She is absolutely present and we can feel her breathing. LX slowly fades to very low light.* ACTOR ONE *enters from centre left. He is playing Joseph.* JOSEPH *steps away from* MARIAN. ACTOR ONE *steps into his place and takes up the same position with* MARIAN. *A tableau emerges in the half-light. The picture freezes. Snap blackout. Snap lights up. Bright wash.* JOSEPH *is standing downstage left, regarding the tableau, as before; now he becomes the reviewer, he is in the act of reviewing the scene.* **MARIAN** *and* **ACTOR ONE** *appear lifeless, even as they are caught in the frozen picture.* **JOSEPH** *begins to write in his notebook. Snap blackout (2). VX goes dark.*

Pause.

LX atmospheric, theatrical, but overexposed, as when old film footage is about to flame out. VX footage of de Valera's 1935–1936 commemoration of the Rising. Snatches of audio begin to be heard. It is Eamon de Valera's "The Ireland that we Dreamed Of" speech from 1943, discordant at first but coming through clearly if intermittently as the SX loops the first three minutes of that speech and it rises and falls with the action and pauses. **ACTOR ONE** *and* **MARIAN** *are no longer on stage. The scene is unchanged. We hear the rattling of a cart. It is pulled onstage by* **ACTOR TWO**. *He places the cart centre stage, he is cantankerous at the task he has to perform, and it shows. He sits down, at the front of the cart, normally reserved for the horse. Enter* **The Countess Cathleen** *and the* **Old Woman**. *They move downstage right and left of the cart, respectively. They move in the same physical language as before. When they are in position, enter* **ACTOR ONE** *as* **MACDARA**.[8] *MACDARA moves to cart and stands on it. He regards the audience. He seems to diminish the women.*

Pause.

MACDARA speaks:

> "I will talk to your souls more strangely yet."

> (*To* **The Countess Cathleen** *and to the* **Old Woman**)

> "You did not do your work well enough." (**The Countess Cathleen** *turns from him, travelling further downstage right*)

> "You should have kept all back but one." (*The* **Old Woman** *turns from him, travelling further downstage left*)

Now, to the audience, **MACDARA** *begins to raise his arms till he is in cruciform by the end of these lines, house lights flicker briefly and go out as he says his lines.*

> "One man can free a people as one Man redeemed the world. I will take no pike. I will go into battle with bare hands. I will stand up before the Gall as Christ hung naked before men on the tree."[9]

Tableau. De Valera's speech can be heard plainly and then recedes. Pause. Tableau ends. **MACDARA** *begins his speech again. As he does so, he begins to take his clothes off.* **JOSEPH** *enters from stage left and hurries to* **MACDARA**, *stopping him from taking off his clothes.* **ACTOR ONE** *stops on command.*

JOSEPH (*jovial, and trying to cover his embarrassment at the thought of the* **ACTOR ONE**'s *stripping his clothes off*)

No, No!... No need. No need!

JOSEPH *turns to his audience, he is about to give his review of what all have just seen. Yet, now, he decides to talk to the audience awhile. All* **ACTORS** *relax and become themselves; they get stools from offstage and sit around or on the cart chatting to each other while* **JOSEPH** *talks to the audience. It's as if they are in rehearsal and are having a break. They are used to* **JOSEPH** *dropping in and at times they react to what* **JOSEPH** *is saying, at other times they are not interested.*

JOSEPH (*speaks to the audience; he moves about the stage freely as he does so and at times he speaks of the actors and of the play*)
I am, I find...
"The perfect gentlemen of the old school"
Kind
Ordinary
Malicious
Bigoted
Vituperative

A gossip and a philistine no less

"Not a deep or penetrating critic"

Easily swayed by the opinions of others

An ordinary man with a touch of cleverness,
A unremarkable man with a journal
Who did not ruffle his pages with the fiercer passions (*We feel the ghost of those passions here*)

Well, Well

However, I make no apology as others have done that perfectly well

*He tells the audience of his "**Proclamation of Faith**." **ACTORS** become part of his audience here for some moments; they are interested in what **JOSEPH** has to say of them. They are not above deriding his pride and his ego when it is called for through these lines.*

> I am essentially a man of the theatre
> My description of acting and of actors is my strongest and soundest point
> There, my judgement is pure, my taste impeccable (*checks pride*)
> I admit my standards can shift, but that is for others to penetrate
> I feel most strongly that…. (*Gathers himself*)

> "The criticism of the actor is quite as important and integral as the criticism of the play
> My chronicle then is of the actors and of how well they played their parts"[10]

JOSEPH *regards* **MACDARA** *who, on cue, retakes his position, as do the others in tableau so that* **JOSEPH** *can give his review. We hear de Valera's tones rise and fall here timed through* **JOSEPH's** *conversation with the audience.*

> I have glimpsed this in rehearsal
> I am not convinced of its excellence
> Nor am I as yet, thrown into a tizzy of moral indignation

(*Of* MACDARA)

His is a peculiar, "pistol-shot like delivery," which can,
At times ruin his natural style of playing ...
"He hasn't the gift of sustaining character ...
But of playing himself"
Indeed he may never play any other sort of part

(*Of the* '*Play*')

It will be explosive no doubt
Yet, it can become "trying to listen to after a time"
A great pity
For there is a constant danger
Of falling into artificial playing
Which can ruin a player's art

(*Regards the scene for a moment, then back to the audience*)

You know a play must always build up the interest from the rise
of the curtain
And always keep the interest on the move ...
Well, well, this may prove so[11]

(**JOSEPH** *prepares to leave the stage; he remembers one last thing, which he must tell
the people*)

They said I would not mind being tidied up by other people,
People after me
People cleverer than I ...
I do mind you know

(*Takes one last look at* **MACDARA** *and the others who, having relaxed the
tableau, make one last exasperated gesture to hold the picture. They really
want him to leave*)

Mmmm ... I'll drop by again tomorrow

JOSEPH *begins to exit downstage right. As he does so, VX of* **MARIAN***, fills
the screens as backdrop. The VX is blurred; we catch one clear glimpse of her.
She speaks, and the VX holds for a few moments before blurring out again.*

MARIAN   My name is Marian Culler

SX Loud to fill the room, and repeated to sound like a cacophony of different women's voices saying
My name is Marian Culler

SX stops abruptly VX of Marian **MARIAN** *taking a breath*)

JOSEPH (*walking towards the image of* **MARIAN**)

Rehearsing I presume?
Snap Blackout
The End

NOTES

1. Games of Lamentation.
2. All instances of quoted material for the character of The Countess Cathleen are sourced from W.B. Yeats, *The Countess Cathleen*, https://www.gutenberg.org/files/5167/5167-h/5167-h.htm.
3. All quoted material for the character of JOSEPH is sourced from *Joseph Holloway's Abbey Theatre: A Selection from His Unpublished Journal Impressions of a Dublin Playgoer*, ed. Robert Hogan and Michael J. O'Neill (Illinois: Southern Illinois University Press, 1967), pp. 6–7.
4. This line also belongs to the play *The Countess Cathleen*. I have used it for MARIAN in the play and amended for that purpose as bricolage. See W.B. Yeats, *The Countess Cathleen*, https://www.gutenberg.org/files/5167/5167-h/5167-h.htm.
5. All instances of quoted material for the character of the Old Woman are sourced from W.B. Yeats, Cathleen ni Houlihan, in *The Collected Works in Verse & Prose of William Butler Yeats*, https://www.gutenberg.org/files/49611/49611-h/49611-h.htm#Page_31.
6. All instances of quoted material for the character of The Countess Cathleen are sourced from W.B. Yeats, *The Countess Cathleen*, https://www.gutenberg.org/files/5167/5167-h/5167-h.htm.
7. All quoted material for the character of JOSEPH is sourced from *Joseph Holloway's Abbey Theatre: A Selection from His Unpublished Journal Impressions of a Dublin Playgoer*, ed. Robert Hogan and Michael J. O'Neill (Illinois: Southern Illinois University Press, 1967), pp. 50–1.
8. From Pádraic Pearse's play *The Singer*, https://celt.ucc.ie//published/E950004-001/index.html

9. All instances of quoted material for the character of MACDARA are sourced from Pádraic H. Pearse, *The Singer*, https://celt.ucc.ie//published/E950004-001/index.html.

10. The work of this section of text is sourced through direct full quote, or as partial quote amended to work as a lines of script, or as paraphrase, and is from Hogan and O'Neill's "Introduction" in *Joseph Holloway's Abbey Theatre: A Selection from His Unpublished Journal Impressions of a Dublin Playgoer*, ed. Robert Hogan and Michael J. O'Neill (Illinois: Southern Illinois University Press, 1967), pp. xi–xxiii.

11. The work of this section of text is sourced through direct full quote, or as partial quote amended to work as a lines of script, or as paraphrase, and is from Hogan and O'Neill's "Introduction" and from the main body of the work as bricolage in *Joseph Holloway's Abbey Theatre: A Selection from His Unpublished Journal Impressions of a Dublin Playgoer*, ed. Robert Hogan and Michael J. O'Neill (Illinois: Southern Illinois University Press, 1967).

BIBLIOGRAPHY

CHAPTER TWO—POPULAR THEATRE IN IRELAND

Booth, Michael R. 1991. *Theatre in the Victorian Age.* Cambridge: Cambridge University Press.

Brooks, Peter. 1995. *The Melodramatic Imagination: Balzac, Henry James, Melodrama, and the Mode of Excess.* Yale: Yale University Press.

Colleary, Susanne. 2015. *Performance and Identity in Irish Stand-Up Comedy: The Comic 'I'.* Hampshire: Palgrave.

de Búrca, Séamus. 1983. *The Queen's Royal Theatre Dublin 1829–1969.* Dublin: Séamus de Búrca.

Fitz-Simon, Christopher. 2011. *Buffoonery and Easy Sentiment: Popular Irish Plays in the Decade Prior to the Opening of the Abbey Theatre.* Dublin: Carysfort Press.

For the Land They Loved: Irish Political Melodramas 1890–1925, ed. Cheryl Herr (Syracuse: Syracuse University Press, 1991).

Foster, R.F. 2015. *Vivid Faces: The Revolutionary Generation in the 1890–1923.* UK: Penguin Random House.

Hogan, Robert, and Richard Burnham. 1984. *The Art of the Amateur 1916–1920.* Portlaoise: Dolmen Press.

Jackson, Vikki, 2010. *Gags and Greasepaint: A Tribute to Irish Fits-Ups,* ed. Mícheál Ó hAodha. Newcastle upon Tyne: Cambridge Scholars Publishing.

Krause, David. 1982. *The Profane Book of Irish Comedy.* London: Cornell University Press.

© The Author(s) 2018
S. Colleary, *The Comic Everywoman in Irish Popular Theatre,*
Palgrave Studies in Comedy,
https://doi.org/10.1007/978-3-030-02008-8

Levitas, Ben. 2002. *The Theatre of Nation: Irish Drama and Cultural Nationalism 1890–1916*. New York: Oxford University Press.

McFeely, Deirdre. 2012. *Dion Boucicault: Irish Identity on Stage*. Cambridge: Cambridge University Press.

Morash, Christopher. 2002. *A History of Irish Theatre, 1601–2000*. Cambridge: Cambridge University Press.

Rahill, Frank. 1967. *The World of Melodrama*. Philadelphia: Pennsylvania State University Press.

Ryan, Philip B. 1998. *The Lost Theatres of Dublin*. Wiltshire: Badger Press.

Trotter, Mary. 2001. *Ireland's National Theaters: Political Performance and the Origins of the Irish Dramatic Movement*. Syracuse: Syracuse University Press.

Watt, Stephen. 1991. *Joyce, O'Casey and the Irish Popular Theatre*. New York: Syracuse University Press.

———. 2004. Late 19th Century Irish Theatre: Before the Abbey—And Beyond. In *The Cambridge Companion to Twentieth-Century Irish Drama*, ed. Shaun Richards. Cambridge: Cambridge University Press.

CHAPTER THREE—COMIC TEXTS

Bourke, P.J. 1991a. When Wexford Rose. In *For the Land They Loved: Irish Political Melodramas 1890–1925*, ed. Cheryl Herr. Syracuse: Syracuse University Press.

———. 1991b. For the Land She Loved. In *For the Land They Loved: Irish Political Melodramas 1890–1925*, ed. Cheryl Herr. Syracuse: Syracuse University Press.

Whitbread, J.W. 1991a. Lord Edward or '98. In *For the Land They Loved: Irish Political Melodramas 1890–1925*, ed. Cheryl Herr. Syracuse: Syracuse University Press.

———. 1991b. Wolfe Tone. In *For the Land They Loved: Irish Political Melodramas 1890–1925*, ed. Cheryl Herr. Syracuse: Syracuse University Press.

CHAPTER FOUR—COMIC WOMEN (SOME MEN ARE ALSO INVOLVED)

Aston, Elaine, and Ian Clarke. 1996. The Dangerous Woman of Melvillean Melodrama. *New Theatre Quarterly* 12 (45): 30–42.

Bakhtin, Mikhail. 1984. *Rabelais and His World*, Trans. Helene Iswolsky. Bloomington: Indiana University Press.

Berger, Peter. 1997. *Redeeming Laughter: The Comic Dimension of Human Experience*. Berlin: Walter De Gruyter.

Bristol, Michael. 1989. *Carnival and Theatre: Plebeian Culture and the Structure of Authority in Renaissance England*. New York: Routledge.

Brooks, Peter. 1995. *The Melodramatic Imagination: Balzac, Henry James, Melodrama, and the Mode of Excess*. Yale: Yale University Press.

Carlson, Susan. 1991. *Women in Comedy: Rewriting the British Theatrical Tradition*. Ann Arbor: University of Michigan Press.

Colleary, Susanne. 2015. *Performance and Identity in Irish Stand-Up Comedy: The Comic 'i'*. Hampshire: Palgrave.

Critchley, Simon. 2002. *On Humour, Thinking in Action*. Oxon: Routledge.

Dean, Joan Fitzpatrick. 2004. *Riot and Great Anger: Stage Censorship in Twentieth Century Ireland*. Wisconsin: University of Wisconsin.

Double, Oliver. 2012. *Britain Had Talent*. Oxon: Palgrave.

Eltis, Sos. 2013. *Acts of Desire: Women and Sex on Stage 1800–1930*. Oxford: Oxford University Press.

Farley-Hills, David. 1981. *The Comic in Renaissance Comedy*. Basingstoke: Macmillan Press.

Finney, Gail. 2014. Little Miss Sunshine and the Avoidance of Tragedy. In *Gender and Humour: Interdisciplinary and International Perspectives*, ed. Delia Chiaro and Raffaella Baccolini. Abingdon: Routledge.

Foster, R.F. 2015. *Vivid Faces: The Revolutionary Generation in the 1890–1923*. UK: Penguin Random House.

Lachmann, Renate, Raoul Eshelman, and Marc Davis. 1988–1989. Bakhtin and Carnival: Culture as Counter—Culture. *Cultural Critique* 11: 124–130.

Meaney, Geraldine. 1991. *Sex and Nation; Women in Irish Culture and Politics*. Dublin: Attic Press.

Meaney, Geraldine, Mary O'Dowd, and Bernadette Whelan. 2013. *Reading the Irish Woman: Studies in Cultural Encounter and Exchange, 1714–1960*. Liverpool: Liverpool University Press.

Morash, Christopher. 2002. *A History of Irish Theatre, 1601–2000*. Cambridge: Cambridge University Press.

Morreall, John. 1987. A New Theory of Laughter. In *The Philosophy of Laughter and Humour*, ed. John Morreall. New York: State University of New York.

Nelson, Robin. 2013. *Practice as Research in the Arts: Principles, Protocols, Pedagogies, Resistances*, ed. Robin Nelson. Hampshire: Palgrave.

Nikulin, Dmitri. 2014. *Comedy, Seriously: A Philosophical Study*. New York: Palgrave.

Newey, Katherine. 1997. Melodrama and Metatheatre: Theatricality in the 19th Century Theatre. *Journal of Dramatic Theory and Criticism* 12 (1): 87.

Peacock, Louise. 2014. *Slapstick and Comic Performance: Comedy and Pain*. Basingstoke: Palgrave.

Reynolds, Paige. 2007. *Modernism, Drama, and the Audience for Irish Spectacle*. Cambridge: Cambridge University Press.

Schechner, Richard. 1985. *Between Theater and Anthropology*. Philadelphia: University of Pennsylvania Press.

Stott, Andrew. 2005. *Comedy*. Oxon: Routledge.

Trotter, Mary. 2001. *Ireland's National Theaters: Political Performance and the Origins of the Irish Dramatic Movement*. Syracuse: Syracuse University Press.

Weitz, Eric. 2016. *Theatre and Laughter*. London: Palgrave.

CHAPTER FIVE—THE COMIC EVERYWOMAN

Bailey, Gilli Bush. Putting It into Practice: The Possibilities and Problems of Practical Research for the Theatre Historian. *Contemporary Theatre Review*. https://doi.org/10.1080/1086800208568697.

Eltis, Sos. 2013. *Acts of Desire: Women and Sex on Stage 1800–1930*. Oxford: Oxford University Press.

Fitz-Simon, Christopher. 2011. *Buffoonery and Easy Sentiment: Popular Irish Plays in the Decade Prior to the Opening of the Abbey Theatre*. Dublin: Carysfort Press.

For the Land They Loved: Irish Political Melodramas 1890–1925, ed. Cheryl Herr (Syracuse: Syracuse University Press, 1991).

Graham, Colin. 2001. *Deconstructing Ireland; Identity, Theory Culture*. Edinburgh: Edinburgh University Press.

Morash, Christopher. 2002. *A History of Irish Theatre, 1601–2000*. Cambridge: Cambridge University Press.

Ó hAodha, Micheál. 2011. *"Insubordinate Irish," Travellers in the Text*. Manchester: Manchester University Press.

Siddons, Henry. 1822. *Practical Illustration of Rhetorical Gesture and Action; Adapted to the English Drama; From a Work on the Subject by M. Engel, Member of the Royal Academy of Berlin*.

Watt, Stephen. 1991. *Joyce, O'Casey and the Irish Popular Theatre*. New York: Syracuse University Press.

Women in Irish Drama, ed. Melissa Sihra (Palgrave: Basingstoke, 2007).

CHAPTER SIX—CLOSE IN

Colleary, Susanne. 2015. *Performance and Identity in Irish Stand-Up Comedy: The Comic 'I'*. Hampshire: Palgrave.

Index[1]

[1] Note: Page numbers followed by 'n' refer to notes.

© The Author(s) 2018
S. Colleary, *The Comic Everywoman in Irish Popular Theatre*,
Palgrave Studies in Comedy,
https://doi.org/10.1007/978-3-030-02008-8

CPSIA information can be obtained
at www.ICGtesting.com
Printed in the USA
LVHW072315060119
602961LV00016B/358/P